REDEEMING SUNDAR

Faith and Innovation in the Age of AI

By Dr. Noah Manyika

A project of

the
issachar
coll3ctive
ENVISION · BUILD · TRANSFORM
978-1-965649-13-8

Table of Contents

Author Testimonials

"When Noah Manyika speaks, it's hard not to be transfixed."

Mary Wong - *President*
Office Depot Foundation

"One of the most gifted communicators I know... rare deep intellect and ability to connect with audiences of all types."

Jay Hein – *CEO*
Sagamore Institute

"A leader of leaders in a class of his own...inspiring master coach with unique abilities to educate and dissect micro and macro issues on a global scale."

Manny Ohonme – *Founder/CEO*
Samaritan's Feet & The World Shoe

"An outstanding orator and brilliant thought leader on global issues and trends. I have heard him hold many audiences in Washington, D.C. spellbound."

Dr. Allan Goodman - *President*
International Institute of Education (IIE)

Reviews of Previous Published Work

Reviews of "The Challenge of Leadership: Is There Not a Cause?"

"This book has the inspirational edge of a Dale Carnegie piece and the moral and spiritual backbone of the book of James. It is a sermon on leadership, not a theoretical, ivory tower polemic. It is a must read for anyone attempting to be a leader and for those who sense the need to lead but lack the courage to do so!"

Julian Champion – *Founder*
West Point School of Music, Chicago Il.

"An excellent work...one of the two best I have ever read on Christian leadership. Noah thank you for enduring the process and writing of it."

Steve Martin - *Director*
Derek Prince Ministries.

"Powerful work...Noah has offered superb clarity and discernment on the way God regards the leadership issue, both in Christian and secular circles."

Dennis Matangira – *Senior Managing Partner Zebu Investment Partners.*

"Powerful reading. At a time when the church desperately needs leaders at all levels, Noah Manyika, with much insight and wisdom, has written a critically important book. It is extremely biblical. It is practical. It is real. It will change the lives of those who have a calling to spiritual leadership."

Byron Wicker – *Senior Pastor RiverLife Fellowship, NC.*

"With the applied logic, craftsmanship and inspired passion reminiscent of the classical artisan and follower of Christ who crafted the New Testament argument that Christ was the promised Messiah, Manyika challenges us to make the essential connection between unconditional submission and mission, and to rise to the virtue of availability."

Dr. Jameson Kurasha – *Professor Religion, Classics and Philosophy*

Praise for "Redeeming Sundar: Faith and Innovation in the Age of AI"

"With the digital world advancing at such a rapid pace, *Redeeming Sundar* is a masterful and powerful call to action, inspiring believers to lead with wisdom, creativity, and unwavering commitment to Kingdom values."

DeAngelo Burse - *Professor,*
TEDx and Keynote Speaker & Author

"The majority of the church is living in denial, settling into a worrisome irrelevance that separates faith from science. It is time for the church to heed Jesus' brutal critique that the children of this world are wiser in their generation than the sons of light. If we are to engage the world, we need language for believability - and this is what this powerful book generously provides."

Dr. Oladotun Reju - *Professor*
Transformational Leadership.
Bakke Graduate University, Dallas, TX.

"With profound insight and clarity, Dr. Manyika masterfully bridges the worlds of faith and innovation, challenging readers to see technology not as a threat, but as a powerful tool for advancing the Kingdom of God. *Redeeming Sundar* is an essential guide and must read for anyone with a passion to see the flourishing of God's Kingdom in an ever-changing world."

> **Rev. Tapiwa Nduna** – *Founder*
> *Bread of Life International Ministries, UK.*

"As a Christian leader in international development, I am deeply challenged by Noah's call to integrate faith and innovation. This book offers Biblically rooted actionable insights for effecting socioeconomically transformative faith-driven innovation. We can no longer separate technological progress from our spiritual mandate to transform lives."

> **Dr. Komborero Choga** – *Senior Director*
> *Compassion International.*

"The men of Issachar were known for their wisdom and understanding of the times. Noah Manyika is one of them. Disruptive technology has been a constant challenge to navigate for faith leaders throughout history. *Redeeming Sundar* will profoundly inspire you to embrace emerging technologies while remaining grounded in the fundamental Great Commission mandate."

Rev. Michelle Hoverson – *Founder*
Lake Norman CDC, NC, USA.

"Dr. Manyika boldly and compellingly advocates for integrating faith and innovation from a biblically grounded perspective. His unique insights draw from a remarkable multidisciplinary journey - including life behind the Iron Curtain in Romania, studies at Georgetown under leaders like Madeleine Albright, advanced degrees from Bakke and Vision universities, and diverse experiences as pastor, missionary, entrepreneur, CEO, and 2018 Zimbabwe Presidential Candidate. This book is essential reading for anyone committed to bridging faith and technology for Kingdom advancement and human flourishing."

Dr. Gwen Dewey – *ex President*
Bakke Graduate University, Dallas, TX

"This work is more than a polemic on technology and its usage. It is a call to arms for the church to rise up a little higher and seize the opportunities before us to use all means possible to preach the gospel of the Kingdom of God to the four corners of the globe. I highly recommend the book you find in your hands and the overall ministry of Dr. Noah Manyika, a visionary and apostle for our time and season."

Dr. Stan DeKoven – *President*
Vision International University, USA.

"*Redeeming Sundar* is an outstanding and exceptionally well-written book. It provides innovative, practical insights and effective strategies for overcoming internal and external obstacles in navigating a world where rapidly accelerating technology reshapes our lives in ways that once seemed purely futuristic."

Byron Wicker – *Senior Pastor*
RiverLife Fellowship, Mooresville, NC.

"I've known Noah for more than twenty years. Several things remain consistent with him. He lives and breathes leadership. He tries to understand the geopolitics surrounding us today. He is amazingly innovative. And he wants to find out new ways to reach and serve people for the Lord Jesus who guides his life. With *Redeeming Sundar* he proves once again that his work is always worth reading. You'll certainly know more and be better because of it."

David Chadwick - *Senior Pastor*
Moments of Hope Church, Charlotte, NC.

REDEEMING SUNDAR

Faith and Innovation in the Age of AI

Imagine not just learning to live within the context of a whole new set of emergent conditions but leading others to embrace these shifts in their own lives. This is the fundamental leadership task – dealing with the same changes as everyone while helping others thrive in a new reality.

Quantum Leadership

Acknowledgements

The pandemic from 2020 to 2023 offered a rare gift: time. Time to reflect, reevaluate, and discern my life's work. These years marked a pivot into a significant new chapter, built upon three decades of personal, professional, and scholarly experiences.

I am deeply thankful for my wife, Phillis Manyika (née Mugabe), who embodies my late mother's final words in 2013: **"Do everything that the Lord has gifted and assigned you to do."** Phillis carries these words with me, continually reminding me of them and walking alongside me through every adventure. Her love, support, and insightful editing of my thoughts and writings are invaluable. Together with our incredible children Danielle, Rahab, and Tinayeshe Kennedy, she makes my work possible.

Our family's journey as missionaries in Charlotte, North Carolina since 1995 shaped the heart of this book. We are grateful for those who served alongside us through the House of David Worship Center, Nexus Church, Nexus Global Serve, and

Hope Junction. These ministries sparked initiatives like Brookstone Schools, the Charlotte Children's Fund, and an inner-city robotics program later adopted by Charlotte Mecklenburg Schools. Each of these experiences informed my earlier book, *The Challenge of Leadership: Is There Not a Cause?*, and this current work.

In 2023, I co-founded Kitchen Copilot Inc. with Scott Forsyth, a man of great faith and technical brilliance. This AI-powered meal planning and health integration app combines my passions for food, technology, and ethical entrepreneurship, illustrating the principles of faith and innovation explored in this book.

My journey at Bakke Graduate University, where I pursued a Doctorate in Transformational Leadership, helped me clarify and organize my ideas on transformational, faith-driven entrepreneurship, culminating in the Prevail Model for Sustained Social Innovation - the subject of my next book. This experience laid the foundation for empowering others to boldly act at the intersection of faith and innovation.

This book is more than a reflection - it is a launching point for the future. Its publication coincides with the launch of *The Issachar Coll3ctive*, a faith-driven innovation and impact platform inspired by 1 Chronicles 12:32. The Coll3ctive aims to catalyze technology-powered solutions to global challenges, reflecting God's care for every aspect of life.

I look forward to speaking at your board retreat, Sunday School, conference, or visiting your marketplace endeavors, where faith in action truly manifests. May this book inspire bold action at the intersection of faith and technology.

Special thanks to Eddie Jones (writerscoach.us) for expertly shepherding this manuscript to publication readiness. To my family, collaborators, mentors, and friends - this work stands on your shoulders.

Dr. Noah Manyika
Charlotte, NC, USA
February 2025

Take Courage

History whispers of fears undone,
Of battles fought and victories won.
Through trials faced, humanity blooms,
Finding strength to forge paths anew.
It brought not chaos, but hope instead,
Advancing life where fear had fled.
So, faithful hearts, take courage anew,
The God of all holds the future too.

Noah Manyika - January 2025

PROLOGUE
The Whisper, the Fork, and the Future

"If you look at the various strategies available for dealing with a new technology, sticking your head in the sand is not the most plausible strategy."
Ralph Merkle - Computer Scientist

The Whisper That Won't Be Silenced

In the quiet moments of life, when the noise fades and thoughts wander, there's a stubborn whisper that stirs in the hearts of many faithful: *Is our faith safe in the age of AI?*

Visions of artificial intelligence (AI) as a tsunami of uncontrollable power - one so immense that even God might be unable to contend with it - are fed by uninformed claims about what it can do, lack of understanding about what it is, or its advent as a sudden imposition on humanity.

But history reminds us that humanity has often faced similar fears, counterbalanced by remarkable hope. Take 1983, at the height of the Cold

1

War. The United States launched the Strategic Defense Initiative (SDI), a high-tech program aimed at intercepting ballistic missiles. Critics derided it as "Star Wars," a fantastical impossibility. Yet by 1988, President Reagan confidently announced the program's technological feasibility, describing its rapid advancements and their broader implications for medicine, air traffic control, and computing. His only lament? The barriers were no longer technological but political.

The fears of the faithful, much like the skepticism surrounding SDI, are heightened when confronted with something unfamiliar. It feels overwhelming - like a tsunami - if we don't recognize that AI is not a sudden phenomenon but a development decades in the making.

A History of Innovation

Artificial intelligence, as a term, is already 69 years old, coined by John McCarthy in 1956 during the Dartmouth Summer Research Project on Artificial Intelligence. This pivotal event marked the formal birth of AI as a field of study. Yet the idea of machines that can "think" predates McCarthy, stretching back to antiquity's study of logic and formal reasoning. These intellectual traditions laid the groundwork for the first computers in the 1940s and the many efforts to build what early visionaries called an "electronic brain."

Few moments in this timeline stand out as much as the "Mother of All Demos." On December 9, 1968, Douglas Engelbart, an American engineer and inventor, presented the oN-Line System (NLS) at the ACM/IEEE Computer Society's Fall Joint Computer Conference in San Francisco. His live, 90-minute demonstration introduced features that now define modern computing: windows, hypertext, graphics, the computer mouse, word processing, video conferencing, and more. This event transformed the future of technology, influencing operating systems of the 1980s and 1990s and establishing the foundations of today's digital world.

Engelbart's demonstration underscores an important truth: technological revolutions are rarely abrupt. They are the culmination of years of quiet, determined work by visionaries who see beyond the present. For the faithful, this raises an essential question: *Will we be overwhelmed by the future, or will we help shape it?*

Faith and Technology: A Divine Gift

Technology, when viewed through the lens of faith, can reveal itself as a gift from God. Consider Israel's Iron Dome, an advanced air-defense system powered by AI. Its speed, accuracy, and intelligence protect lives daily. For Israel, the Iron Dome represents not just human ingenuity but a tool of divine providence, a reminder that technology can serve a higher purpose when aligned with godly values.

Yet, too often, the faith community views technology with suspicion, failing to see its potential for good. This book challenges that perspective. It invites believers to embrace the same boldness that David showed when confronting Goliath - a courage rooted in trust, preparation, and action.

Facing the Tsunami of Change

The fears surrounding AI echo the wisdom of Ecclesiastes:

"For man also does not know his time: Like fish taken in a cruel net, Like birds caught in a snare, So the sons of men are snared in an evil time, When it falls suddenly upon them." (Ecclesiastes 9:12)

The snare is not the technology itself but our failure to anticipate and prepare. When we wake up to its complexity, it can feel overwhelming, even evil. Yet this fear is not rooted in truth. Technology, like any tool, reflects the values of those who wield it. Paranoia alone will not stop its disruptiveness.

What the faith community must grapple with is how to prepare for seismic societal shifts. Consider LinkedIn co-founder Reid Hoffman's prediction: the traditional 9-to-5 job could be a thing of the past within the next decade. If this becomes reality, how will the faith community respond? How will it lead in helping people navigate this transformation, ensuring stability, purpose, and a sense of belonging in an era of unpredictable change?

The challenge is not to resist change but to rise above fear and take proactive steps to shape the future in alignment with Kingdom values. The faith community has a unique opportunity to guide society through this upheaval, demonstrating that technology, when wielded wisely, can reflect divine justice, creativity, and compassion.

The Fork in the Road

This book is a call to reclaim the Church's historical role as a leader in innovation and culture. It challenges the faithful to stop asking, *Is our faith safe?* and instead embrace the opportunity to leverage AI and other technologies for the Kingdom of God.

Ronald Reagan once suggested that the greatest challenges to the SDI program were political, not technological. For the Church, the greatest barrier is a mindset of paranoia and misinformation that inhibits bold action. This book invites readers to move beyond fear and into informed faith, recognizing this moment as a divine invitation to innovate, lead, and build.

A Glimpse of What's to Come

This book will take you on a journey through the critical questions and challenges facing faith communities in the age of AI. It's a call to leaders, innovators, and everyday believers to rise to the moment with informed faith and bold action. In the chapters ahead, you'll wrestle with profound ideas, such as:

- **Whispers and Warnings:** How do we discern fear-mongering from legitimate caution, and what role does faith play in navigating the unknown?
- **The Proactive Kingdom:** What does it mean for believers to lead the charge in innovation, rather than reacting to disruptions?
- **Faith at the Speed of Life:** How to integrate timeless truths with modern realities, empowering individuals and communities to thrive.
- **Foolproofing:** How to leverage technology and AI to build resilience against future challenges and disruptions.
- **The Theology of Giftedness:** How can the unique talents God has given you contribute to shaping the future?
- **Godlikeness vs. Godliness:** How do we balance our pursuit of excellence and creativity with humility and reliance on God?

- **Building the Future:** What will it take for the Church to become a hub of creativity and transformation in a world hungry for hope?

Each chapter is designed to provoke thought, inspire action, and equip you to embrace your role as a builder of systems, communities, and ideas that reflect God's justice, mercy, and beauty.

The Journey Ahead

In the pages that follow, you'll find a roadmap for navigating the age of AI with faith as your compass. You'll meet the "whisperers" who stoke fear about technology and learn how to replace their whispers with informed faith. You'll explore a proactive vision for believers shaping the future rather than reacting to it. And you'll uncover how your unique talents can contribute to God's redemptive work in the world.

This is not a call to retreat but a rallying cry to advance. It's time to think bigger, dig deeper, and step boldly into the future, confident that God is already there, waiting to partner with us.

The Church stands at a crossroads. Will we retreat into irrelevance or rise to lead and transform? The choice is ours. The whisper has become a call. The fork in the road lies before us. The future awaits.

Welcome to *Redeeming Sundar*. The journey begins now.

"Men often oppose a thing merely because they have had no agency in planning it, or because it may have been planned by those whom they dislike."

Alexander Hamilton - U.S. Founding Father

CHAPTER 1
Satan's Trap: The Whisperer

"Now a word was brought to
me stealthily; my ear received
the whisper of it."
Job 4:12

The latest warning of impending apocalypse arrived in the form of a question, as cryptic and unsettling as those before it: "Did you know that Nutella was born into a Telugu Hindu family in 1967 in Hyderabad, India, and that his mother, Parabati, was an expert in Sanskrit, the sacred language of Hinduism?"

The Whisperer, oblivious to the mangled name, was undeterred in his oracular mission to warn against "the horned ones." Satya Narayana Nadella, the India-born CEO of Microsoft, had become Nutella, and his mother, Prabhavati, was now Parabati. These errors of detail didn't matter. To the Whisperer, their names alone—strange, foreign, unpronounceable—were evidence enough of a sinister conspiracy.

The Whisperer's warnings were not new. Over the years, they had emerged from different voices, bound by a shared conviction that advanced technology was a harbinger of Armageddon. This time, the horned ones were tech leaders like Satya Nadella, NVIDIA's Jensen Huang, and Alphabet's Pichai "Sundar" Sundararajan—figures who, according to the Whisperer's righteous indignation, had coaxed the tools of science fiction into everyday life to herald humanity's downfall.

My last name might have lumped me with these supposed villains, but my first name, Noah, a nice Judeo-Christian name, suggested we shared a common faith, that I could therefore be trusted with these revelations which needed to be whispered to prevent these bad people from hearing through the ubiquitous gadgets they had created that we were on to them.

Allow me a digression: I was born in Southern Rhodesia during the days of the Central African Federation. My middle name, Ngoni, (which would be my first name today but for the social pressures of the times for natives to have "Christian" names) actually means "The mercy/grace of God." By some perverse colonial logic, Ngoni did not qualify as Christian and would most likely have been viewed with suspicion by the Whisperer decades later because it is not an English name!

The Whisperer I am concerned about is not a person who merely warns about the dangers of technology. Neither is it an individual, but successive characters I have encountered over the years who believe they have a calling to put fear into The Body of Christ. They include the visitor to my office in 1999 during the countdown to Y2K or that moment when the "wicked" binary code would finally deal humankind its ultimate comeuppance.

The electric grid was going to fail. High-tech planes were going to fall out of the sky, and worse: the computers controlling the launch of nuclear weapons would go rogue, triggering a nuclear conflagration that would end civilization as we knew it. The visitor claimed God had assigned them to remind me of my leadership responsibility not just to protect my family, but the congregation I led from the coming apocalypse. What was unsaid was clear: God would hold me accountable for what happened to my family and the people I led if I did not do the right thing.

More than just the whispered warning was delivered by The Whisperer who also brought a Y2K survival kit of battery-powered lanterns, portable gas stoves and other things we never used and have since donated to Goodwill.

Can technology be dangerous in the wrong hands? Of course. But why is it more likely to end up in the wrong hands than under the control of people who are ethical and will use it responsibly? Part of this is the technophobia which can paralyze people of the Christian faith at critical times in human history. The goal of this work is not just to encourage our nominal presence as technology breaks new ground and defines new possibilities of doing life, but to inspire us to be compelled by our faith to be the conscientious instigators of tech and social revolutions that positively impact humanity.

Proverbs 18:8 warns that the words of a whisperer "are like delicious morsels" which "go down into the inner parts of the body." At this critical juncture in human history, we have to be careful to feed our souls with words that don't feed our paranoia. The same bible that encourages us to be sober and vigilant (1 Peter 5:8) also reminds us that God did not give us a spirit of fear, "but of power, and of love and of a sound mind" (2 Timothy 1:7). Allowing the soft, stealthy, persistent reminders of mankind's technological Armageddon by the whisperers to feed our collective paranoia can dissuade people of faith from reskilling, ensuring that despite the Lord giving us all things pertaining to life and godliness (2 Peter 1:3-4), we will be left behind.

It is critically important in the 21st century for the faith community to not focus only on spiritual literacy to achieve godliness, but to also recognize the urgent need to be literate in matters pertaining to life. As Alvin Toffler, the renowned futurist, aptly observed: "The illiterate of the 21st century will not be those who cannot read and write, but those who cannot learn, unlearn, and relearn." This perspective aligns with the call to continually renew our minds (Romans 12:2), allowing us to navigate a rapidly changing world without compromising our faith.

In Chapter 10, we will discuss in more depth the importance of faith that integrates godlikeness and godliness, redeeming humanity through creativity, humility, and transformative power. To embody this faith is to reflect the fullness of God's design for humanity - fully human, fully alive, and wholly committed to glorifying God in all things. This requires holistic literacy, encompassing spiritual, intellectual, and cultural adaptability.

I contend that Christianized or spiritualized paranoia is still paranoia. The same jaundiced view of history that would dismiss Ngoni as a Christian name would most likely view the ascension of a Nadella to the helm of Microsoft or Sundararajan to the CEO's office at Google (Alphabet) as an invasion of the Christian domain by Easterners and Third World aliens with malicious intent. Such attitudes not only foster unhelpful division but also undermine the global mission of faith—to embrace adaptability and innovation as reflections of God's creative plan for humanity.

There are good reasons to be vigilant. The reality is that in the 21st Century, technology companies have also amassed unprecedented economic power, giving them immense influence over how we all do life. Four of the five largest companies by market cap in the world today (Apple, Inc., Microsoft Corp, Saudi Aramco, Amazon Inc., Alphabet Inc.) are technology companies with valuations exceeding a trillion dollars. Microsoft is a behemoth whose June 2024 market cap stood at $3.352. To put its scale and influence in relation to the US economy into perspective, its valuation represents 12.25% of the United States' GDP of $27.36 trillion. It is perfectly understandable to be concerned that a company's market cap can represent as large a percentage of a modern, diversified economy's GDP as Microsoft does today (12.25% of the world's largest economy) whether it is run by a William "Bill" Henry Gates III whose family regularly attended a Congregational Church in his youth, or by someone born into a Telugu Hindu family in 1967 in Hyderabad India whose mother (Prabhavati) was an expert in Sanskrit, the sacred language of Hinduism.[1]

Nadella's counterparts at NVIDIA and Alphabet, the parent company of Google have origins in the same region and lead companies that wield just as much economic and technological

---

[1] Sanskrit is defined by the Oxford Languages Dictionary as "an ancient Indo-European language of India, in which the Hindu scriptures and classical Indian epic poems are written and from which many northern Indian (Indic) languages are derived." It is the sacred language of Hinduism and was key to the spread of Hindu and Buddhist culture in the Southeast, East and Central Asia.

power. Jen-Hsun "Jensen" Huang, born in Tain-an City, Taiwan leads NVIDIA, June 2024 Market Cap: 3.105T. As of June 25, 2024, Alphabet (Google's parent company) led by Pichai Sundararajan, better known as Sundar Pichai and born in Madurai, Tamil Nadu, India had a market cap of $2.28 trillion.

For the ordinary consumer, daily interactions with technology often justify concern. Alexa, for example, does seem to be always listening. While having it as a personal assistant to control our lights, radios, and other devices offers convenience, it comes with notable downsides. Similarly, Siri is listening too, sometimes responding like a precocious or overly intrusive child, answering questions that were never directed to it. That's a problem. It also seems far from coincidental when we're suddenly bombarded with ads for products we discussed privately with friends or loved ones but never searched for online. These experiences should concern everyone, not just people of faith.

For people of faith, however, there is an additional danger: the assumption that we can engage with technology in blissful and pious ignorance, thinking we do not need to understand how it works. Yet, like everyone else, we are deeply dependent on it. A lack of understanding makes it difficult to discern which functionalities to accept or reject—beyond the basic utility that serves us well without causing harm. Navigating these complexities requires a thoughtful, informed approach to determine how technology can enhance life while avoiding unnecessary risks.

Yes, some of the threats posed by new technologies are real and serious. However, withdrawal is not the answer—nor is it feasible, given how significantly technology has improved our lives and work. Instead, we must take an active role in leading innovation, building ethical guardrails to limit abuse, and mitigating the dangers that technology may pose to humanity. At the same time, we should celebrate the privilege of living in an era when, by God's grace, humanity has been gifted with the ability to dream - and build - solutions as big as, or even bigger than, the critical problems we face. The contributions of today's innovators, including the Sundars of our time, are a testament to God's generosity in granting creativity and ingenuity to all.

Discussion Questions

1. **The Whisperer's Perspective:**
   - How does the portrayal of "The Whisperer" challenge or affirm the way you approach new technologies as a person of faith?
   - Why do you think fear is often the default reaction among some Christians when confronted with technological advancements?
   - How does the concept of technophobia connect to the biblical warnings against paranoia (e.g., Proverbs 18:8, 1 Peter 5:8)?

2. **Cultural and Historical Bias:**
   - How does the colonial dismissal of the name "Ngoni" as Christian reflect broader biases in how certain cultures and people are perceived?
   - In what ways do cultural and historical biases shape modern narratives about leadership in tech industries?

3. **Ethical Use of Technology:**
   - What role should Christians play in ensuring that technology is used ethically?

- Do you agree with the assertion that withdrawal from technology is not the answer? Why or why not?
4. **Faith and Innovation:**
   - How does faith inspire innovation, according to the author?
   - What are some practical ways people of faith can become "conscientious instigators of tech and social revolutions"?
5. **Global Leadership and Diversity:**
   - How does the rise of diverse leaders like Nadella, Huang, and Pichai in technology challenge traditional ideas about faith, nationality, and innovation?
   - How can people of faith celebrate diversity in leadership while maintaining vigilance about ethical concerns?

Practical Exercises

1. **Faith and Tech Reflection:**
   Write a personal reflection on how your faith influences your relationship with technology. Include examples of how you use technology in daily life and how you discern its potential benefits and risks.

2. **Bias Awareness Activity:**
Research the backgrounds of leaders in technology (e.g., Satya Nadella, Jensen Huang, Sundar Pichai). Reflect on how their stories challenge assumptions about who can lead in innovation. Share one way their leadership could inspire you to engage with technology differently.

3. **Technological Audit:**
   - Identify three technologies or tools you use regularly (e.g., Alexa, Siri, social media platforms).
   - Evaluate each for its ethical implications, convenience, and potential risks.
   - Write down steps you can take to ensure you use these tools responsibly.

4. **Group Exercise: Ethical Guardrails for Technology**
   - In a group, brainstorm a set of ethical principles or "guardrails" that should guide Christians in their use and creation of technology.
   - Discuss how these principles can be applied practically in everyday tech interactions or in leadership roles within the tech industry.

5. **Paranoia vs. Vigilance:**
    - Reflect on a time when you felt hesitant or fearful about adopting new technology.
    - Identify whether your hesitation was rooted in justified vigilance or paranoia.
    - What steps could you take to move from fear to informed engagement?
6. **Vision Board: Faith and Innovation**
    - Create a vision board or write a list of ways faith-driven individuals can positively influence the tech industry.
    - Include specific actions, roles, or innovations you believe people of faith can lead to foster ethical and life-enhancing technology.
7. **Scripture Study and Application:**
    - Study the following verses: Proverbs 18:8, 1 Peter 5:8, 2 Timothy 1:7.
    - Discuss how these scriptures can shape a faithful and balanced approach to technology.

"It is not the critic who counts, not the one who points out how the strong man stumbled or how the doer of deeds might have done them better. The credit belongs to the man who is actually in the arena."

President Theodore Roosevelt – Paris, 1910

CHAPTER 2

Let Us Go Up at Once and Possess it!

"Do not wait; the time will never be 'just right.'
Start where you stand, and work with whatever
tools you may have at your command, and
better tools will be found as you go along."
George Herbert – English Poet

Introduction

This book is not specifically about Google CEO Sundararajan "Sundar" Pichai. Nor does it suggest that he is viewed as an archenemy of the Kingdom by the faith community. However, as a leading figure in the technology world, Pichai's name, derived from the Sanskrit *Sundararaja* meaning "beautiful king," serves as a compelling metaphor for the concept of redeeming - or metaphorically, "dehorning Sundar."

Ironically, Pichai shares his first name with Sadhu Sundar Singh, a revered Indian Christian missionary of the late 19th and early 20th centuries.

Sadhu Sundar Singh, often called the "Apostle with the Bleeding Feet," was known for his transformative vision of faith and service, walking the rugged terrains of India to spread the Gospel. While one Sundar exemplified the redemption and beauty of Christ's mission, the other Sundar stands at the crossroads of technology's vast potential and the faith community's cautious engagement with it. This historical parallel deepens the metaphor of "Redeeming Sundar" and challenges us to view the leaders of today's technological revolution through a similar lens of purpose and possibility.

This book is a direct challenge to the faith community to stop reacting and start leading - to be the Calebs of our time. Like Caleb in Numbers 13:30, who confidently declared, "Let us go up at once and possess it, for we are well able to overcome it," we are called to act with certainty in the Lord and trust in the unshakable nature of His promises. It urges the Church to reclaim its place on the frontlines, leading with foresight and faith to shape the future. Moving beyond the reflexive paranoia that often characterizes certain segments of the faith community, this book invites critical discussion. It emphasizes the need for collaborative partnerships between faith and technology to address human needs and advance the Kingdom's work, underscoring that this is not a battle to resist technology, but an opportunity to redeem and steward it for God's purposes.

In the following chapters, I hope to:

1. **Dispel Paranoia:** Remove the "horns" often assigned to innovators who are unjustly demonized as agents of unchecked technological disruption. By dismantling these myths, we can reframe such individuals as contributors to humanity's progress.

2. **Humanize Innovators:** Portray innovators as human beings with God-given gifts, strengths, and flaws, and as individuals fulfilling a divine role in shaping the future.

3. **Reclaim Perspective:** Offer a perspective rooted in biblical truth, helping the faith community move beyond reactionary fears of technology to acknowledge both its challenges and opportunities.

4. **Bring Faith into the Future:** Encourage the faith community to engage courageously and wisely with technological advancements such as AI, shaping the future alongside innovators.

The Peril of Passive Faith

Fear, when left unchecked, paralyzes even the most well-intentioned communities. In Chapter 1, we explored how whispers of technological doom often deter believers from embracing tools and opportunities that God has provided. Similarly, adopting a passive stance toward the world's challenges reduces the Kingdom of God to a reactive force.

Redeeming Sundar signifies rejecting the portrayal of innovators as "the horned ones" - or metaphorically, dehorning them. This concept offers a lens to understand the paralysis that fear induces. Too often, leaders at the forefront of technological innovation are reflexively cast as "horned ones," demonized as agents of chaos. Yet this narrative stems from misplaced paranoia, overlooking the God-given creativity and purpose these individuals carry.

Proverbs 22:3 reminds us: "The prudent see danger and take refuge, but the simple keep going and pay the penalty." This verse is not mere advice - it is a call to proactive stewardship. The Church must be more than a caretaker of traditions; it must act as a watchtower, anticipating challenges, seizing opportunities, and shaping the future.

Passivity allows others to dominate spheres of influence—technology, governance, science, and more—often to the detriment of godly principles. To dehorn Sundar is to replace unfounded fear with informed faith and proactive engagement.

The Wisdom of Proactive Readiness

The parable of the Ten Virgins (Matthew 25:1–13) warns of the consequences of complacency. The wise virgins prepared their lamps in advance, while the foolish ones, unprepared, were shut out of the wedding feast. Jesus' admonition to "keep watch" underscores the need for vigilance—not only in spiritual matters but also in addressing the pressing challenges of today.

Similarly, Ezekiel 33:6 warns spiritual leaders who fail to act when danger looms:

"If the watchman sees the sword coming and does not blow the trumpet, the people will perish, but their blood I will require at the watchman's hand." This call to vigilance challenges the Church to reject passivity and embrace its role as a forward-looking community.

Dehorning Sundar means recognizing that innovators are not harbingers of chaos by default,

33

but contributors to humanity's ability to thrive amid change. It is not innovation itself that should be feared but rather our failure to engage with it as a tool for God's purposes.

Understanding the Times: Lessons from the Sons of Issachar

The "sons of Issachar" in 1 Chronicles 12:32 were commended for their understanding of the times and wisdom to act accordingly. In a world of accelerating technological and cultural shifts, this insight remains as relevant as ever.

A few years ago I was working on Fundo, a remote learning platform which a friend I was seeking support from dismissed as a "solution looking for a problem." Its true value became undeniable during the pandemic, which underscored the importance of such tools. Similarly, the Church often struggles to anticipate future needs, finding itself reactive rather than proactive.

This work calls the faith community to adopt the foresight of the sons of Issachar. Instead of vilifying innovators, we must learn from their ability to anticipate, innovate, and act. These leaders live as though the future is already here, reshaping industries and society with urgency and vision.

A Disrupted Work Reality

LinkedIn co-founder Reid Hoffman's daring prediction that the traditional 9-to-5 workday will disappear by 2034 adds urgency to the Church's need to adopt foresight and leadership. As AI advances and the gig economy flourishes, Hoffman envisions a future where stable, predictable work structures give way to fragmented, flexible arrangements.

Hoffman's forecast has profound implications:

- **For the Institutional Church**: Many churches rely on the predictability of the traditional work week to structure Sunday services and mid-week fellowships. If schedules become increasingly irregular and people no longer gather in a single geographic place, churches will need to offer more flexible, decentralized, and virtual options to remain relevant.
- **For Families**: The 9-to-5 model has provided families with stability in finances and time. Its disappearance could disrupt rhythms

of connection, create economic instability, and lead to new pressures on relationships. Churches must provide resources to help families navigate these changes.

- **For Individual Christians**: Fragmented work could lead to isolation, anxiety, and a loss of purpose. However, it also opens doors for believers to integrate faith into diverse callings. The Church has a pivotal role in equipping individuals to thrive in this new reality.

This work invites the faith community to anticipate these changes and lead by example, ensuring that innovation serves humanity and reflects God's redemptive purposes.

Commandoes Jump into Strongholds

Passivity comes at a cost. The Church's withdrawal from key areas of influence has allowed secular ideologies to dominate:

- **In Academia:** Without faith-driven voices, Christian students often face environments that are hostile to their beliefs.
- **In Leadership:** Proverbs 29:2 reminds us, "When the righteous are in authority, the

people rejoice; but when the wicked rule, the people groan." Abandoning leadership creates a vacuum that is often filled by rulers who oppose godly values.

- **In Technology:** Avoiding innovation cedes ground to those who may wield tools like AI for harm rather than good.

Kingdom advancement will not happen by merely being vocal about being at war and claiming to have weapons that are "mighty through God to the pulling down of strong holds" (2 Corinthians 10:4) while failing to actively reclaim those vacated spaces. Reclaiming these spaces requires both courage and a willingness to dismantle the myths that hinder engagement.

Redeeming Sundar is about more than humanizing innovators - it's about recognizing that their work, when stewarded ethically and creatively, can align with God's purposes. President Theodore Roosevelt's "Man in the Arena" speech, delivered in Paris, France, on April 23, 1910, offers a fitting challenge:

"It is not the critic who counts; not the man who points out how the strong man stumbles, or where the doer of deeds could have done them better. The credit belongs to the man who is actually in the arena, whose face is marred by dust and sweat and blood; who strives valiantly; who errs, who comes short again and again, because there is no effort without error and shortcoming; but who does actually strive to do the deeds; who knows great enthusiasms, the great devotions; who spends himself in a worthy cause; who at the best knows in the end the triumph of high achievement, and who at the worst, if he fails, at least fails while daring greatly, so that his place shall never be with those cold and timid souls who neither know victory nor defeat."

As Roosevelt observes, nothing extraordinary is accomplished by those who fear failure. The call to reclaim vacated spaces is a summons to enter the arena—to dare greatly, strive valiantly, and align innovation and leadership with God's purposes, regardless of the cost.

Overcoming Fear and False Dichotomies

In Chapter 1, we addressed the paranoia that often stifles Christian engagement with technology. Now, we turn to the faith community's kingdom responsibility to reject the false dichotomies between sacred and secular- divisions that have hindered the Kingdom's advance for too long. When these divides are left unchallenged, critical spaces are ceded to narratives that distort God's truth:

- **In Medicine**: Viewing it as secular leaves the throne of healing vacant, inviting Asclepius, the Greco-Roman god of medicine, to occupy it.
- **In Science**: If God is not acknowledged as Creator, Urania, the goddess of astronomy, assumes dominion over discovery.
- **In Sports**: Without recognizing God as the source of victory, Nike, the goddess of triumph, takes the place of honor.
- **In Politics**: The faith community's absence allows Zeus, Poseidon, and Hades to vie for power.
- **In Culture**: When faith abandons domains like sexuality and creativity, figures like Aphrodite and Anat shape narratives that distort God's truth.

The faith community must reject these dichotomies and embrace its call to integrate faith into every sphere of life. By doing so, we ensure that God's presence and truth permeate all areas of human activity, offering hope and guidance to a world in need.

Practical Steps for Proactive Leadership

To reclaim leadership, the faith community must:

1. **Embrace Foresight**: Equip leaders to anticipate opportunities and challenges, like the sons of Issachar.
2. **Engage Courageously**: Actively participate in shaping the future of technology, governance, and culture.
3. **Commit to Innovation**: Lead in creating ethical, faith-driven solutions to modern problems.
4. **Celebrate God's Work Through Humanity**: Recognize advancements as reflections of God's gifts to humanity.

A Unified Call to Action

The Kingdom of God is not reactive - it shapes the future. Fear and nostalgia have no place in a community called to lead with faith, wisdom, and innovation. Redeeming Sundar is a rallying cry to dispel myths, overcome fears, and reclaim a bold, proactive vision for engaging with technology and culture.

Reid Hoffman's prediction about the end of the traditional workday is a wake-up call. The Church must anticipate these changes, adapt its methods, and take decisive steps to lead. This includes re-thinking how we gather, how we support families in a fragmented work environment, and how we equip individuals to navigate a rapidly evolving world.

The Proactive Kingdom embraces change not with hesitation, but with hope. It calls us to shape the workplace, the home, and the community to reflect God's justice, mercy, and beauty. By stewarding tools like AI with discernment, the Church has the opportunity to inspire transformation and offer a future rooted in purpose and belonging.

Discussion Questions

On Fear and Leadership

1. What are the potential implications of Reid Hoffman's prediction for the traditional

9-to-5 workday on the institutional church, families, and individual Christians?

2. What role does fear play in the faith community's reluctance to engage with technology and innovation?

3. How does the metaphor of "Dehorning Sundar" reshape the faith community's perspective on leaders in technology?

4. In what ways does passive faith hinder the Kingdom's work in technology, culture, and governance?

Biblical Insights

5. How do the lessons from Proverbs 22:3, the parable of the Ten Virgins (Matthew 25:1–13), and Ezekiel 33:6 challenge the Church to adopt a proactive approach?

6. What can the modern Church learn from the sons of Issachar in 1 Chronicles 12:32 about anticipating and responding to cultural and technological shifts?

Reclaiming Vacated Spaces

7. The chapter discusses the Church's withdrawal from areas like academia, technol-

ogy, and politics. Which of these areas do you think requires the most immediate action from the faith community, and why?

8. How can the Church overcome the false dichotomy between sacred and secular to integrate faith into all spheres of life?

Engaging with Innovators

9. Why is it important to humanize technological innovators rather than demonize them?

10. How can recognizing innovation as a reflection of God's creativity inspire the faith community to engage with modern challenges?

Practical Exercises

Personal Reflection

1. **Tech and Faith Inventory:**
   - List the technologies you use daily.
   - Reflect on how these tools impact your spiritual life and community engagement.
   - Identify one way you can use technology to advance the Kingdom's work.

2. **Understanding the Times:**
   - ◦ Study 1 Chronicles 12:32 in its historical and biblical context.
   - ◦ Write down how the concept of understanding the times applies to a modern challenge you or your community face.

Group Activities

3. **Debate Exercise:**
   - ◦ Split into two groups. One group argues why fear of technology is justified, while the other argues why proactive engagement is essential.
   - ◦ After the debate, discuss how a balance between vigilance and engagement can be achieved.
4. **Vision Mapping:**
   - ◦ In a group, identify one "vacated space" (e.g., technology, academia, politics) where the faith community can lead.
   - ◦ Brainstorm actionable steps to reclaim influence in that space.

Foresight and Planning

5. **Foresight Journal:**
   - Choose a technological trend (e.g., AI, renewable energy, biotechnology).
   - Research its potential societal impact and write a journal entry outlining how faith-driven leaders can guide its ethical development.
6. **Parable Study:**
   - Revisit the parable of the Ten Virgins (Matthew 25:1–13).
   - Identify "oil" you need in your "lamp" to be prepared for opportunities or challenges in your sphere of influence.

Practical Engagement

7. **Ethical Innovation Plan:**
   - Develop a one-page proposal for a technology or innovation that aligns with godly values.
   - Include potential challenges and how you would address them from a faith-driven perspective.

8. **Reclaiming Cultural Influence:**
   - Identify a cultural or societal narrative where faith perspectives are underrepresented.
   - Create a plan to influence that narrative through a project, campaign, or initiative.

"The heart of him that hath understanding seeketh knowledge: but the mouth of fools feedeth on foolishness."

Proverbs 15:14

CHAPTER 3

Defining AI: Understanding the Age of Artificial Intelligence

"...the sons of Issachar...had understanding of the times, to know what Israel ought to do.."

Proverbs 22:3

Introduction

The Age of AI has arrived at a time of great mistrust and polarization. On one side is a tech industry that often views faith as regressive or irrelevant. On the other, a faith community wrestling with concerns about the ethical ramifications of technological advancements it perceives as encroaching on humanity's moral boundaries.

Into this cauldron of mistrust steps Artificial Intelligence, a transformative technology that both excites and unsettles. Understanding AI and its implications requires addressing not only technical questions but also the cultural and relational dynamics between faith and innovation. Before delving into what AI is and is not, let's examine Proverbs 15:14 and its relevance to this discussion.

A Lot of Life Beyond Gathering: Why We Seek Knowledge

The Kingdom does not advance by limiting life to gatherings or religious experiences. Proverbs 15:14 tells us, "The heart of him that hath understanding seeketh knowledge: but the mouth of fools feedeth on foolishness." At the heart of the Christian experience is the gift of understanding, which opens the eyes of the believer to the deeper *"why"* of creation and existence. This understanding transforms the search for knowledge from a pointless pursuit into a meaningful quest to engage the world effectively, ethically, and redemptively.

Scriptures like Ecclesiastes 12:12 - "And further, by these, my son, be admonished: of making many books there is no end; and much study is a weariness of the flesh" - are sometimes misused to justify a lack of intellectual curiosity and engagement with knowledge. However, 2 Timothy

2:15 underscores the need for a diligent pursuit of knowledge: "Study to shew thyself approved unto God, a workman that needeth not to be ashamed, rightly dividing the word of truth." Nowhere does this imply that study should be limited solely to aspects of the Word of Truth that pertain to godliness, nor that knowledge relevant to life and its practicalities is unimportant.

There is much life beyond gatherings or dramatic religious experiences. In Matthew 17, when Jesus led Peter, James, and John up a high mountain - believed by some to be Mount Tabor in Israel - they witnessed Christ's transfiguration: "His face shone like the sun, and His clothes became as white as the light. And behold, Moses and Elijah appeared to them, talking with Him" (verses 2–3). Peter's response is noteworthy: "Then Peter answered and said to Jesus, 'Lord, it is good for us to be here; if You wish, let us make here three tabernacles: one for You, one for Moses, and one for Elijah.'"

The phrasing in the NKJV -"Then Peter answered"- is intriguing because no question was asked. Peter essentially told Jesus, "Lord, it is good for us to be here." Similarly, when the faith community insists on operating only within the boundaries of knowledge permitted by its religious rituals and traditions, it is, in effect, telling God what is good for it to do or not to do. Yet, we were not created to erect tents where we witness Jesus' transfiguration, nor were we called to passively wait, eyes fixed on the skies, for Christ's return after His ascension.

In Acts 1:11, the message from the two men in white apparel - clearly angels - who watched the disciples "looking steadfastly toward heaven as He went up" could not have been clearer: "Men of Galilee, why do you stand gazing up into heaven? This same Jesus, who was taken up from you into heaven, will so come in like manner as you saw Him go into heaven."

We seek understanding of artificial intelligence, the Age of AI, and technology in general because there is a vast life to be lived beyond gatherings, and this knowledge and understanding can be fully leveraged to fulfill both the Creation Mandate in Genesis 1 and the Great Commission in Matthew 28. If the faith community is to leverage emerging technologies for Kingdom advancement and contribute to shaping ethical guardrails for technological development, understanding what these technologies are and how they function is essential. Uninformed criticism weakens the Christian witness, alienating those outside the faith who might otherwise be open to its message.

What Is AI?

Let me begin by defining the Age of AI before delving into a discussion of the technology itself. As noted in the prologue of this book, the term *artificial intelligence* is now 69 years old, having been coined by John McCarthy in 1956 during the Dartmouth Summer Research Project on Artificial Intelligence, an event that marked the formal birth of AI as a field of study. The development of AI has been ongoing since that time.

What I refer to as the *Age of AI*, however, began with the release of ChatGPT in 2022. This milestone marked the transition of AI from being a specialized tool to becoming a global, mass-market phenomenon. It also heightened awareness of AI's potential, sparking a worldwide conversation about its implications and possibilities.

So, what is AI? It refers to systems and technologies that simulate human intelligence, performing tasks such as learning, reasoning, problem-solving, and language comprehension. At its core, AI processes large datasets to identify patterns, make predictions, and execute tasks that traditionally required human input. AI can be classified into three categories: Narrow AI, General AI (AGI), and Superintelligent AI.

The AI we see today falls into the category of Narrow AI, which is designed to perform specific tasks—such as virtual assistants, fraud detection systems, and recommendation algorithms. These systems operate within clearly defined parameters and lack the capacity for generalization or adaptability beyond their intended function.

General AI (AGI), on the other hand, refers to systems capable of performing any intellectual task that humans can. AGI would demonstrate adaptive, self-directed reasoning and problem-solving. With advancements in fields such as quantum computing, AGI is moving from being a speculative concept to a plausible reality, raising both excitement and caution.

The third category, Superintelligent AI, is currently hypothetical. It envisions a stage where AI surpasses human intelligence across all domains. While this remains speculative, discussions about superintelligence underscore the importance of establishing ethical frameworks to guide future technological advancements and ensure that such systems are developed responsibly.

The Context of Distrust

The mistrust between the faith community and the tech industry is rooted in historical, cultural, and practical tensions. Issues such as ethics, privacy, and the societal impact of automation are debated in a polarized environment where both sides often question each other's motives and values.

The faith community is frequently dismissed by the tech industry as out of touch or irrelevant - criticisms that, at times, are not entirely unwarranted. However, this mistrust is compounded by revelations from whistleblowers that suggest the tech industry is not always trustworthy. For instance, some whistleblowers have claimed that certain AI systems exhibit signs of sentience. For a faith community already cautious about technological overreach, the fact that such claims are often refuted by industry insiders rather than independent experts only deepens concerns about transparency and trust.

This mistrust is also indicative of a deeper, systemic issue: the cultural reinforcement of the sacred-secular divide. This divide - often unspoken but deeply ingrained - positions faith as a private, personal matter, rather than an integral part of public and professional life.

The Illusion of Inclusive Workplaces

Mike Robbins' advocacy for employees bringing their "whole selves" to work has been embraced in some modern workplaces. Robbins, the author of *Be Yourself, Everyone Else Is Already Taken: Transform Your Life with the Power of Authenticity*, champions authenticity as a tool to foster collaboration, innovation, and psychological safety within organizations. He encourages individuals to embrace their unique identities, share their perspectives openly, and integrate their personal values into their professional lives.

However, the concept of an inclusive workplace has often been an illusion for many people of faith. They quickly discover that bringing their whole selves to work can lead to alienation and even negative professional repercussions. For instance, during the COVID-19 pandemic, objections to vaccine mandates or health policies voiced by individuals known to be people of faith were frequently dismissed as irrational or extreme. In many cases, such dissenting views - often attributed exclusively to their faith - resulted in damaged reputations and even job losses.

The reality is that workplaces where individuals of faith can truly bring their authentic selves to work are rare. Companies like Applied Energy Services (AES), co-founded in 1981 by Dennis Bakke - a man of faith and author of *Joy at Work* - stand out as exceptions. Bakke and his partners were determined to embed the ethos of their faith into the company's culture, creating a workplace that genuinely valued authenticity and integration of personal values.

The Reality and Risks of AI

The faith community has valid reasons to be concerned, particularly if the tech community's ultimate goal is to create a sentient being. In every era, there are those who are reckless enough to attempt to play God. While I believe it is impossible for humans to create truly sentient beings, AI does not need to achieve sentience to raise significant concerns. Advances in technology - especially with algorithms processing vast amounts of data and the potential of quantum computing - enable AI to mimic human emotions and actions at an unsettling level. As AI progresses toward General AI, the ethical and philosophical implications become increasingly urgent.

Each technological breakthrough comes with inherent risks. For example, early objections to the internal combustion engine (ICE) stemmed from fears that it might explode. The idea of engines relying on controlled explosions of fuel within a cylinder to generate power was a novel and somewhat frightening concept in the late 19th and early 20th centuries. While the greatest risks for mechanical technologies often occur in their early stages, these concerns usually diminish over time as rigorous testing and safety improvements are implemented. Similarly, while we may only be a few years into the Age of AI, the technology itself has been under development for over five decades.

AI, however, presents unique challenges due to the very nature of the technology. Unlike the internal combustion engine, which was created to carry humans, AI is perceived by many as being designed to *be* human. This distinction raises profound questions: What does it mean to be human in an age where machines rival human intelligence? How can we ensure that AGI systems align with ethical principles and respect human dignity? What role should the faith community play in shaping a moral framework for AGI?

While these questions deserve careful attention, I believe the individual reading this book will also benefit from focusing on the tangible opportunities that the Age of AI offers. By embracing these opportunities thoughtfully, we can better navigate this new technological era while addressing its ethical and philosophical challenges.

How Real Are the Opportunities in the Age of AI?

"Let's be real" is a common response when people are challenged to embrace something new. The challenge, however, is that opportunities in the Age of AI can often appear as delusions at worst or vapor at best. Yet, vapor is real. Consider those who dismissed Amazon's early vision - pre-AI but still relevant - as implausible. Its growth, from $0.5 million in revenue in 1995 to $574.8 billion in 2023, with a market capitalization of $2.375

trillion, demonstrates the transformative power of embracing new paradigms.

Opportunities in the Age of AI require a shift in perspective. Beyond resisting the paralysis of fear, people of faith must reconsider what real opportunities look like and reframe their understanding of modern economies. For example, God's answer to a prayer for a new job after being laid off might come in the form of an opportunity that a person of faith does not immediately recognize. That opportunity could involve creating content for a global audience using digital platforms, building a following that attracts brands and advertisers, and unlocking monetization potential.

Unfortunately, platforms like TikTok and Instagram are often dismissed as hubs for viral dances, pranks, or superficial trends. What is overlooked is their role within the rapidly growing creator economy, valued at $250 billion in 2023 and projected to reach $480 billion by 2027. TikTok alone, with 170 million monthly active U.S. users as of 2024, has provided countless creators with revenue through programs like the Creator Fund and Creator Rewards. Similarly, YouTube, with 2.7 billion monthly active users globally and generating $16.75 billion in revenue in the first half of 2024, offers real income streams for millions of creators, reshaping livelihoods in ways traditional economic systems fail to recognize.

The Biggest Opportunity in the Age of AI

In my view, the greatest opportunity in the Age of AI is the empowerment of individuals to fully embrace their identity as creators. It enables people to transcend physical limitations and boundaries, reaching the broadest audiences imaginable. Notably, this is called the *creator economy*, not the *content economy*. I believe the Age of AI allows anyone to envision better and build better.

This empowerment can take many forms, including:

- **Monetizing traditional skills**: Using AI to create workshops, instructional videos, and online sales channels.
- **Elevating professional consulting**: Offering webinars, eBooks, or virtual consulta-

tions, enhanced by AI for scalability and efficiency, and supported by AI-driven marketing tools.

- **Developing educational content**: Leveraging AI tools to enhance production quality and reach wider audiences.
- **Health and wellness coaching**: Using AI-driven tools to create personalized fitness and nutrition plans for clients, enabling scalable solutions.
- **Publishing**: Writing blogs, books, or newsletters with the assistance of AI tools for drafting, editing, and content optimization.
- **Digital product creation**: Developing templates, tools, or apps for niche markets, accelerated by AI-powered design capabilities.

These examples demonstrate how the creator economy, fueled by AI, offers practical, scalable, and passion-driven pathways to generating income. This revolution is reshaping the traditional work paradigm for those who are willing to adapt and seize the opportunities presented by this transformative era.

Conclusion: Toward a New Partnership

AI represents both a challenge and an opportunity. It invites collaboration, demands trust, and requires a commitment to ethical innovation. For the faith community, this is not a time for retreat but for engagement. By thoughtfully embracing AI, we can shape a future that aligns with God's purposes for creation.

The Age of AI calls the Church to lead with wisdom, courage, and hope. It is an opportunity to redefine work, creativity, and collaboration in ways that reflect the divine mandate to steward the earth and its resources. This moment in history is not merely about adapting to change but about actively shaping it for the Kingdom's advancement.

Discussion Questions

1. **Defining AI**:
   - How would you explain the difference between Narrow AI, General AI (AGI), and Superintelligent AI to someone unfamiliar with the technology?

- What are the ethical concerns that arise as we transition from Narrow AI toward AGI, and how should the faith community address these concerns?

2. **The Sacred-Secular Divide**:
   - Mike Robbins promotes "bringing your whole self to work." Why do you think people of faith often find it difficult to do so?
   - How does the sacred-secular divide impact the ability of the faith community to engage constructively with the tech industry?

3. **The Reality and Risks of AI**:
   - Do you believe AI can ever achieve sentience? Why or why not?
   - How do the philosophical implications of AGI challenge our understanding of what it means to be human?

4. **Trust and Mistrust**:
   - In what ways does the mistrust between the faith community and the tech industry reflect broader societal divides?
   - How can people of faith rebuild trust with innovators in the tech industry, and vice versa?

5. **Opportunities for Collaboration**:
   - What are some specific ways the faith community can collaborate with the tech industry to ensure AI technologies promote human flourishing?
   - How might churches use AI to improve their outreach and service to their communities?

Practical Exercises

1. **AI Education Workshop**:
   - Organize a group discussion or workshop in your community to explore the basics of AI, using real-world examples like ChatGPT or virtual assistants. Discuss the potential benefits and risks, encouraging participants to ask questions and share concerns.
2. **Bridging the Divide**:
   - Reflect on the sacred-secular divide in your own workplace or community. Identify one practical way to integrate your faith authentically into your professional or public life without alienating others. Share your experience with a trusted group.

3. **Ethical AI Brainstorm**:
   - With a small group, develop a list of ethical principles that should guide the development and use of AI technologies. Compare these principles with existing frameworks from tech leaders and discuss how faith can uniquely contribute to these guidelines.

4. **Exploring the Culture of Mistrust**:
   - Write down three ways the faith community can build trust with the tech industry and three ways the tech industry can reciprocate. Reflect on how these actions can foster collaboration and mutual respect.

5. **Case Study Analysis – Dennis Bakke's Leadership**:
   - Read excerpts from *Joy at Work* by Dennis Bakke and discuss how his approach to integrating faith into corporate culture could be applied in modern workplaces, particularly in tech-driven industries.

6. **Role-Playing Dialogue**:
   - Conduct a role-play between a faith leader and a tech industry representative discussing the ethical use of AI. Use

this exercise to practice building mutual understanding and identifying shared goals.

7. **Community AI Audit**:
    ○ Conduct an informal "AI audit" in your local church or organization. Identify areas where AI tools (e.g., language translation, accessibility aids, or data analysis) could enhance your ministry or community services. Create a plan for implementation.

The Man with the Hoe

Is this the Thing the Lord God made and gave
To have dominion over sea and land;
To trace the stars and search the heavens for power;
To feel the passion of Eternity?
Is this the Dream He dreamed who shaped the suns
And marked their ways upon the ancient deep?
Down all the stretch of Hell to its last gulf

Edwin Markham

Poet Laureate of Oregon

CHAPTER 4
Shadowboxing isn't a Knockout

"Therefore I run thus: not with uncertainty.
Thus I fight: not as one who beats the air."
1 Corinthians 9:26

Introduction

In Chapter 2, we examined the faith community's need to reclaim foresight and leadership, confronting passive faith and encouraging believers to engage boldly with the complexities of the modern world. In Chapter 3, we defined AI and the Age of AI, equipping readers to respond to both with knowledge and faith. Now, in this chapter, we focus on the practical embodiment of transformative faith.

Paul's metaphor in 1 Corinthians 9:26 provides a vivid picture of faith in action. Faith cannot afford to be a shadowboxing routine, creating the illusion of effort without meaningful impact. Instead, it must be focused, intentional, and transformative.

This critique applies not only to unproductive faith routines but also to how fear and misunderstanding often lead to superficial engagement with innovation and technology. Earlier, we confronted the "whisperers"- voices that stoke paranoia about the dangers of technology without recognizing its potential for good. Shadowboxing, whether in faith or our approach to technology, leaves us flailing in futility instead of engaging with purpose.

From Shadowboxing to Real Engagement

Every day, Bobby shadowboxed.

The young man would step outside and flail his arms at invisible foes, his jabs landing on empty air. Day after day, this routine defined him. While routines can provide comfort, they do not necessarily yield results.

Bobby's story serves as a metaphor for a troubling pattern in the Church today: the tendency to engage in traditions and routines that give the appearance of action without producing meaningful outcomes. This is shadowboxing faith, reminiscent of the Pharisees in Jesus' time, who clung to rituals while neglecting the weightier matters of justice, mercy, and faithfulness (Matthew 23:23).

Faith communities often fall into similar patterns when addressing modern challenges. Instead of engaging with the complexities of technological innovation or societal change, they retreat into repetitive rituals that lack real-world impact. Just as Bobby's punches never landed, the Church's efforts often fail to connect when they are uninformed or misdirected.

George Foreman practiced shadowboxing, as did Mike Tyson. Both fighters - two of the most formidable punchers in boxing history - understood that shadowboxing could never replace the need to land punches in the ring. For them, shadowboxing was preparation. The goal was always the knockout.

Breaking the Routine

When my team arrived in Charlotte, North Carolina, in 1995 to serve as missionaries, we encountered a city celebrated for its livability yet ranked last in upward mobility. It was a place where the faith community appeared stuck in religious routines while neighborhoods and congregations were being reshaped by hyper-gentrification—changes that were far from beneficial for those displaced and, ironically, neither for the churches that were serving them.

Urban planning studies highlighted the city's aggressive "renewal" plans, which created significant investment opportunities for developers but destabilized long-term local residents. Despite this, many faith leaders appeared disinterested in such data-driven research, dismissing it as secular and unspiritual. Instead, they focused on spiritual mapping meetings and rituals, believing these practices would spark city-wide revivals similar to those in Pensacola or Toronto. Unfortunately, these efforts failed to produce the anticipated spiritual revivals.

This disengagement reflects a broader discomfort within the Church when it comes to engaging with the complexities of modern life. Breaking the routine requires informed faith - a faith rooted in knowledge, actionable steps, and the willingness to confront the real battles of our time armed with the tools of the age.

Informed Faith: Bridging Knowledge and Action

Informed faith calls believers to engage with life's realities armed with knowledge, discernment, and the courage to act. Scripture emphasizes this approach:

- **The Israelites at Paran:** God instructed Moses to send leaders to scout the Promised Land (Numbers 13). This act of reconnaissance was not a rejection of faith but an exercise in informed leadership.
- **Jesus' Emphasis on Planning:** In Luke 14:28, Jesus asks, "Suppose you want to build a tower. Wouldn't you first sit down and calculate the cost?" Faith and planning are partners, not opposites.
- **Paul's Exhortation to Study:** In 2 Timothy 2:15, Paul encourages believers to "study to show thyself approved unto God." Study equips the faith community to act wisely and confidently.

Transformative Presence: David and Eliab

The story of David and Eliab at the Valley of Elah (1 Samuel 17) highlights the difference between transformative and impotent presence:

- **Eliab: Present But Paralyzed**
  Eliab, David's eldest brother, was physically present on the battlefield but spiritually ab-

sent. His resentment and inaction revealed a presence marked by bitterness and insecurity. He criticized David yet contributed nothing to the fight against Goliath.

- **David: Present and Transformative**
  David arrived not with empty criticism but with testimony and theology. His confidence stemmed from God's faithfulness:
  "The Lord who rescued me from the paw of the lion and the paw of the bear will rescue me from the hand of this Philistine" (1 Samuel 17:37).
  David's presence transformed the battlefield, bringing victory where fear and paralysis had prevailed.

Eliab, though he looked the part, lacked the heart for the transformative role God required. When the prophet Samuel came to Jesse's house to anoint a new king for Israel, he initially assumed Eliab was the one, saying,

"Surely the Lord's anointed is before Him!" (1 Samuel 16:6). Yet the Lord quickly corrected Samuel:

"Do not look at his appearance or at his physical stature, because I have refused him. For the

Lord does not see as man sees; for man looks at the outward appearance, but the Lord looks at the heart" (1 Samuel 16:7).

Transformative presence is not about appearances. People of faith can look good shadowboxing—creating the illusion of action—while lacking the courage to step into the ring of life. In the 21st century, this challenge is amplified by social media, which provides ample tools for creating alter egos and projecting a façade of heroism. It's possible to look polished on the outside but remain as impotent as Edwin Markham's character in his poem *The Man with the Hoe*.

Markham captures the tragedy of a life disconnected from its divine purpose:

> *"Is this the Thing the Lord God made and gave*
> *To have dominion over sea and land;*
> *To trace the stars and search the heavens for power;*
> *To feel the passion of Eternity?*
> *Is this the Dream He dreamed who shaped the suns*
> *And marked their ways upon the ancient deep?"*

Markham's lament resonates with the challenge of our time: Are we fulfilling our God-given potential, or are we merely playing a part?

Conclusion: From Shadowboxing to Transformative Faith

Faith that fails to connect with real challenges is shadowboxing—it looks active but achieves little. Transformative faith, by contrast, is focused, informed, and bold, engaging the world with purpose and impact.

Call to Action:

To move from shadowboxing to informed presence:

- **Break routines** that provide comfort but yield no fruit.
- **Embrace informed faith,** equipping yourself with the knowledge and tools to act wisely.
- **Be a transformative presence,** bringing testimony, theology, and courage into every space you inhabit.

The battle is before us. Let us show up—not merely in body but with the testimony and theology that can truly transform the world.

Discussion Questions

Understanding the Problem of Shadowboxing

1. How do you see the metaphor of shadowboxing faith reflected in the modern Church? Can you think of specific examples in your community or personal life?

2. In what ways do fear or misunderstanding contribute to the Church's reluctance to engage with societal and technological changes?

3. Reflect on the Pharisees in Matthew 23:23. How can the Church balance tradition with addressing justice, mercy, and faithfulness today?

Breaking the Routine

4. Why do you think faith leaders in the Charlotte example were resistant to data-driven research? How can the Church overcome the stigma that equates practicality with a lack of spirituality?

5. What routines in your personal or faith community's life might be providing comfort without bearing fruit?

Informed Faith and Transformative Presence

6. How does the story of the Israelites at Paran (Numbers 13) illustrate the balance between faith and informed action? Can you relate this to a decision you've faced?
7. Compare and contrast Eliab and David in 1 Samuel 17. What qualities made David's presence transformative? How can you cultivate those qualities in your life?
8. Why is testimony and theology important in addressing real-world challenges? Share an example of how these have informed your decisions or actions.

Call to Action

9. What practical steps can you take to transition from shadowboxing to informed and transformative faith?

10. How can the Church collectively move from reactive routines to proactive engagement with the world's challenges?

Practical Exercises

For Individuals

1. **Shadowboxing Self-Assessment**
   Reflect on your daily faith practices. List activities that you feel are meaningful and impactful versus those that might be routine without fruit. Pray for wisdom and take one step to shift your focus toward meaningful engagement.

2. **Informed Action Plan**
   Identify a current issue in your community or personal life where you feel paralyzed or uninformed. Research the issue thoroughly (e.g., using scripture, data, or expert insights) and write down an actionable step to address it.

3. **David's Testimony Exercise**
   Write down three past experiences where God's faithfulness has been evident in your life. Use these as a foundation to approach

a current challenge with confidence and courage.

For Groups

1. **Eliab vs. David Role-Play**
   Split the group into pairs. One person takes on the role of Eliab (criticism without action), and the other plays David (confidence based on testimony). Discuss how each approach impacts a shared goal and what the group can learn from the exercise.

2. **Community Impact Workshop**
   Identify a pressing issue in your community (e.g., housing, education, or technology ethics). Use scripture and research to craft a strategy for engagement. Present and discuss your plans as a group, and consider ways to act collectively.

3. **Breaking Comfort Routines**
   As a group, brainstorm faith routines that may have become unfruitful. Identify one practice the group can replace with an intentional action plan, such as volunteering, advocacy, or community outreach.

Ongoing Challenge

1. **Transformative Presence Commitment**
   Commit as a group or individually to being a transformative presence in a specific area of your life (e.g., workplace, neighborhood, or family). Document progress, challenges, and testimonies to share during follow-up discussions.

"The illiterate of the 21st century will not be those who cannot read and write, but those cannot learn, unlearn and relearn."

Alvin Toffler - American Writer/Futurist

CHAPTER 5
Back to the Future

*"The real voyage of discovery
consists not in seeking new landscapes,
but in having new eyes"*
Marcel Proust - French Novelist

Introduction

The digital age, marked by rapid advancements in technology and automation, paradoxically calls us to rediscover values and practices from a bygone era. As the gig and creator economies rise, remote work reshapes industries, and traditional notions of lifelong employment dissolve, a revival of entrepreneurial spirit akin to the agricultural age is emerging. For the faith community, these shifts present both a challenge and an opportunity - a chance to reexamine timeless principles and apply them to the complexities of modern life.

Rediscovery, empowerment, and innovation become guiding themes for navigating contemporary challenges while remaining firmly rooted in faith. By embracing these principles, we can live out our calling as co-creators with God, bringing order, creativity, and compassion into a world in flux.

Going Back to Move Forward

The preacher's wisdom in Ecclesiastes 9:11 - "The race is not to the swift nor the battle to the strong, but time and chance happen to them all" - reminds us of the importance of returning to foundational truths to understand the future. The digital age is steering us toward a mindset reminiscent of the pre-industrial agricultural era, when self-reliance and resourcefulness were essential for survival. Farmers cultivated their land, adapted to changing conditions, and managed resources with ingenuity and collaboration. They thrived by embracing uncertainty and relying on their God-given creativity.

Today, the rise of the creator economy, entrepreneurship, and remote work echoes this ethos. Like farmers diversifying their crops to manage risk, modern workers are embracing digital "tent-making" (Acts 18:3) and leveraging multiple income streams through gig work, creative ventures, and e-commerce.

However, just as the *whisperers* described in Chapter 1 stoke fear about innovation, there are voices urging retreat rather than engagement in this new digital landscape. Rooted in a fear of change or distrust of technological leaders, these warnings can paralyze the faith community when action is most needed.

Rather than succumbing to fear, the Church can draw lessons from the past, leveraging technology not only to adapt and thrive but also to provide a moral framework that ensures innovation serves humanity and glorifies God.

Doing Life as Worship

When Jesus confronted the Pharisees, He exposed not only their hypocrisy but also their limited understanding of worship. His question in Luke 14:5- "Which of you shall have an ox or a son fall into a pit, and will not immediately pull him out on the Sabbath?" - challenged the notion that observing rituals was more important than saving lives.

This teaching reminds us that true worship integrates the sacred and the practical. An ER doctor saving a life on the Sabbath is no less engaged in worship or glorifying God with their gifts than someone singing hymns in a church pew. Their diligence and care reflect the heart of God, just as Abel's offering in Genesis 4:4 did.

God's original design in Eden was holistic: life itself was worship, and humanity's stewardship of creation was an act of devotion. That explains why, according to 2 Peter 1:3, God gives us "all things that pertain to life and godliness." The call to "do life as worship" requires integrating our faith into every aspect of being and doing, whether parenting, working, or innovating.

Rediscovering Values from a Bygone Era

The **Proverbs 31 woman** is celebrated as virtuous not merely for her moral uprightness or religious rituals but for her entrepreneurial and industrious spirit. She offers a compelling example of doing life as worship, demonstrating how faith can be seamlessly integrated into daily work, family life, and economic activity.

Before describing her as "a woman who fears the Lord" in verse 30, the text outlines her many qualities, painting a picture of a life lived with purpose, creativity, and stewardship. Let's consider these traits in detail:

1. **Entrepreneurial Spirit**

   "She considers a field and buys it; out of her earnings, she plants a vineyard" (v. 16). This woman is an entrepreneur who evaluates opportunities, invests wisely, and ensures her ventures bear fruit. Her work is strategic and forward-looking, demonstrating resource stewardship and planning.

2. **Industrious Nature**

   "She selects wool and flax and works with eager hands... In her hand she holds the distaff and grasps the spindle with her fingers" (vv. 13, 19). Far from idleness, her industrious nature serves her household and community, reflecting the biblical principle that diligence leads to abundance (Proverbs 21:5).

3. **Provision for Her Household**

   "She gets up while it is still night; she provides food for her family and portions for her female servants" (v. 15). Her care extends beyond basic needs, embodying leadership through service.

4. **Marketplace Influence**

   "She makes linen garments and sells them, and supplies the merchants with sashes" (v. 24). She actively contributes to the economy, engaging in commerce with skill and ingenuity.

5. **Wisdom and Compassion**

   "She speaks with wisdom, and faithful instruction is on her tongue" (v. 26). Her words guide and build others, while her generosity reflects God's heart: "She opens her arms to the poor and extends her hands to the needy" (v. 20).

6. **Strength and Dignity**

   "She is clothed with strength and dignity; she can laugh at the days to come" (v. 25). She faces the future with confidence, knowing her diligent preparation and trust in God provide security.

7. **Fear of the Lord**

   "Charm is deceptive, and beauty is fleeting; but a woman who fears the Lord is to be praised" (v. 30). Her faith anchors her work, relationships, and ambitions in God's eternal purposes.

Rediscovering the Power of One

Breakthroughs often begin with individuals who embrace responsibility and innovation. Paul's declaration in Philippians 4:13 - "I can do all things through Christ who strengthens me" - underscores the importance of a personal connection with God. This empowerment is not for selfish gain but for serving families and communities.

Proverbs 13:22 reminds us: "A good man leaves an inheritance for his children's children." This legacy, made possible through faith and innovation, reflects God's desire for His people to build, create, and multiply.

Throughout history, revolutions in thought, industry, and technology have been initiated by individuals with a clear understanding of their responsibility to act. The response this work seeks to inspire does not require a collective movement. Instead, it calls for modern-day Davids and Deborahs - those who hear the call of the cause and act decisively. Like Sundar Pichai, Elon Musk, and Jeff Bezos, who are reshaping the world through innovation, these individuals have the opportunity to leave a redemptive mark on humanity.

The Testing

The digital age is leading people of faith into unfamiliar and challenging spaces -territories where the Church has not always equipped them to thrive. For instance, many Christian families find themselves unprepared when the primary breadwinner loses their job due to downsizing. This financial instability often sparks crises within households, contributing to divorce rates within the Church that tragically mirror those in secular society.

Proverbs 31:16 describes the virtuous woman: "She considers a field and buys it." She does not depend on a single income stream but instead cultivates diverse sources of livelihood. Her life demonstrates mastery of multiple skills and a holistic approach to life's challenges. She embodies the principle of being a *Jill of many trades and a master of life.*

Renowned management consultant and educator Peter Drucker encapsulated this mindset when he stated, "The only skill that will be important in the 21st century is the skill of learning new skills. Everything else will become obsolete over time." The Proverbs 31 woman exemplified this long before Drucker's time, living a life of resourcefulness, adaptability, and faith. Her example remains a timeless blueprint for how people of faith should navigate today's complexities.

This kind of *life mastery* - applying God's wisdom to every challenge and vocation - is essential for the faith community. It calls for resilience and the Davidic ability to encourage oneself in the Lord, as described in 1 Samuel 30:6. Especially during times of distress, when external support may be scarce, such vocational and spiritual fortitude is critical for overcoming adversity and thriving.

The Proverbs 31 woman, about whom it is written, "She girds herself with strength and strengthens her arms" (v. 17), illustrates this principle. Her strength is not for selfish individualism but for the benefit of her family and community. Her productivity is a testimony to the God who refreshes and sustains His people, as highlighted in Acts 3:19: "Times of refreshing come from the presence of the Lord."

True mastery enables believers to balance productivity with renewal. As Proverbs 3:7 - 8 states: "Do not be wise in your own eyes; fear the Lord and turn away from evil. It will be healing for your flesh and refreshment for your body." Holistic investment, particularly in family and community, brings true refreshment that empowers continued service.

Conclusion: Redeeming the Past, Building the Future

The digital revolution is not merely a moment of disruption but an invitation to reclaim the entrepreneurial spirit of generations past. As jobs become less secure, we are called to move forward by looking back - to a time when creativity, resilience, and innovation were cornerstones of livelihood.

By rejecting fear and paranoia, as emphasized in Chapter 1, the faith community can prepare its members for the challenges of the modern economy while upholding timeless values. Jesus modeled practical compassion, showing that worship and service are inseparable. In the age of AI, innovation becomes an act of faith, pulling people out of pits and offering hope.

The call is clear: Redeem the past, harness the present, and build a future that honors God and serves humanity. Just as the Proverbs 31 woman embraced the tools of her time, we too must rise to the occasion, leveraging every resource to advance God's purposes and bring abundant life to all.

Discussion Questions

On Rediscovery and Innovation

1. How does the rise of the gig and creator economies reflect the entrepreneurial spirit of the agricultural era?
2. What timeless values from past generations should the Church rediscover to navigate the digital age effectively?
3. How does the concept of "digital tent-making" align with biblical principles of work and provision?

On Doing Life as Worship

4. In what ways does the idea of "doing life as worship" challenge traditional views of faith and work?

5. How does the Proverbs 31 woman model a holistic integration of faith, work, and service?
6. What practical steps can faith communities take to encourage members to view their daily activities as acts of worship?

On Resilience and Mastery

7. How does the Proverbs 31 woman demonstrate resilience and resourcefulness in the face of uncertainty?
8. Why is it important for believers to diversify their skills and income streams in today's economy?
9. How can the Church better equip families to navigate financial instability and other modern challenges?

On Redeeming the Past and Building the Future

10. How can faith communities help their members embrace the tools of the digital age without fear?
11. What role does innovation play in advancing God's purposes and serving humanity?

12. How does the example of individuals like Sundar Pichai and the Proverbs 31 woman inspire believers to lead and create in transformative ways?

Practical Exercises

Personal Reflection

1. **Rediscovering Entrepreneurial Values:**
   - Reflect on how you or your family embody the values of resourcefulness, creativity, and resilience.
   - Write down one way you can further develop these qualities in your daily life.
2. **Life as Worship Audit:**
   - List your daily activities and assess how they reflect God's purposes.
   - Identify one task you can approach more intentionally as an act of worship.

Group Activities

3. **Proverbs 31 Case Study:**
   - Break into groups and analyze the qualities of the Proverbs 31 woman.

- Discuss how these traits can be applied in modern contexts, such as entrepreneurship, gig work, or innovation.
4. **Digital Tent-Making Brainstorm:**
    - As a group, identify examples of modern "tent-making" opportunities (e.g., freelancing, e-commerce, digital content creation).
    - Discuss how these can align with faith and provide for both individual and community needs.

Strategic Planning

5. **Community Innovation Project:**
    - Identify a challenge in your local community (e.g., unemployment, housing, education).
    - Develop a plan that uses modern tools and resources to address this challenge while integrating biblical principles.
6. **Skills for the Future Workshop:**
    - Organize a workshop to help members of your faith community develop skills for the gig economy or digital age.

- ◦ Include topics like financial literacy, entrepreneurship, and technology use.

Visioning and Implementation

7. **Generational Legacy Plan:**
   - ◦ Reflect on Proverbs 13:22.
   - ◦ Create a vision for how you can leave a legacy—spiritually, financially, or relationally—that impacts future generations.
8. **Redeeming the Digital Revolution:**
   - ◦ Imagine a faith-driven digital platform or tool that addresses a pressing societal need (e.g., housing, education, healthcare).
   - ◦ Outline its features, purpose, and how it can reflect God's values.

Resilience and Renewal

9. **Building Resilience Exercise:**
   - ◦ Identify areas of your life where you feel unprepared for challenges (e.g., financial instability, career changes).
   - ◦ Write down steps you can take to strengthen your resilience and prepare for the future.

10. **Balancing Productivity and Renewal:**
    ○ Reflect on Proverbs 3:7–8 and Acts 3:19.
    ○ Develop a plan to balance work, rest, and spiritual renewal in your life.

"We are able to go up and
take the country,
And possess the land from
Jordan to the sea;
And, though giants tall be
there our way to hinder,
God will surely give the victory."
F.W. Suffield - Author and Hymnist

CHAPTER 6
When Faith is Left Behind

"God gave us the gift of life;
It is up to us to give ourselves
the gift of living well."
Voltaire - French Writer/Satirist

Introduction

The urgency of our times calls for faith communities to transform into centers of empowerment for holistic human agency. This transformation hinges on understanding that God gave us the gift of life to live fully. Living fully requires a balanced understanding of the symbiosis of godlikeness and godliness - a harmony we will explore further in a later chapter. Authentic works of faith and testimonies that advance the Kingdom are grounded in this balance, ensuring faith is never left behind in our quest to live abundantly for the glory of God.

When Faith is left in Kadesh Barnea

In Numbers 13, we see a striking example of what happens when faith is left behind. The ten spies sent by Moses, on God's orders, to survey the land of Canaan brought back a dystopian report rooted in fear rather than faith. They declared, "We were like grasshoppers in our own sight, and so we were in their sight" (Numbers 13:33). This story serves as a cautionary tale about the dangers of leaving faith behind when faced with challenges.

Chosen Leaders, Faltering Faith

Let's first examine who these men were, why they were chosen for this mission, and why we would expect all twelve - not just Joshua son of Nun and Caleb son of Jephunneh - to carry their faith with them. To understand Israel's leadership corps at this stage, we turn to Numbers 11, where Moses lamented the overwhelming burden of leadership. God responded by instructing Moses:

"Gather to Me seventy men of the elders of Israel, whom you know to be the elders of the people and officers over them...I will take of the Spirit that is upon you and will put the same upon them; and they shall bear the burden of the people with you." (Numbers 11:16-17)

Moses obeyed, and God fulfilled His promise. The Spirit that rested upon Moses was placed on the seventy elders, and "when the Spirit rested upon them, they prophesied, although they never did so again" (Numbers 11:25). This final clause is crucial: they prophesied when the Spirit came upon them, "although they never did so again." Was this prophetic act meant only to confirm their commissioning? Or was it intended to be an enduring capacity?

In another part of the narrative, Eldad and Medad, two chosen elders who had remained in the camp instead of going to the tabernacle, began to prophesy. This prompted Joshua, described as one of Moses' "choice men" (Numbers 11:28), to urge Moses to forbid them. Moses replied:

"Are you zealous for my sake? Oh, that all the Lord's people were prophets and that the Lord would put His Spirit upon them!" (Numbers 11:29, NKJV)

The NKJV renders Moses' response as "Are you zealous for my sake?" while the NIV translates it as "Are you jealous for my sake?" The distinction here is subtle but significant. Joshua's reaction stemmed from a desire to protect Moses' leadership. He viewed the prophesying of Eldad and Medad as a potential challenge to Moses' authority. However, Moses' response redirected the focus to the larger picture: the purpose of prophecy was not about preserving hierarchical leadership but about empowering more people to serve God's purposes. Moses made it clear that the greater need was for God's Spirit to be poured out broadly, enabling more people to hear Him and walk by faith.

Moses' words underscore an essential lesson for faith leaders: leadership is not about safeguarding positions or structures but about equipping others to live out their calling. The Spirit's work was meant to extend beyond institutional boundaries, allowing the gift of prophecy to serve and guide God's people collectively.

This dynamic is especially relevant today, as technology democratizes knowledge and empowers individuals. Such democratization aligns with biblical affirmations of shared inheritance and calling:

"The Spirit Himself bears witness with our spirit that we are children of God, and if children, then heirs - heirs of God and joint heirs with Christ..." (Romans 8:16-17).

"But you are a chosen people, a royal priesthood, a holy nation, God's special possession, that you may declare the praises of him who called you out of darkness into his wonderful light." (1 Peter 2:9)

When faith communities resist this democratization and limit their influence to religious rituals within houses of worship, they vacate places of broader societal impact. This creates a void that others - *Sundars* of our times, inspired by their God-given creativity and sense of responsibility - step in to fill. These individuals embrace the task of solving humanity's challenges, often without institutional backing, demonstrating a profound engagement with their godlikeness.

The purpose of this work is to challenge the faith community to embrace its responsibility fully. Calling, choosing, and anointing are not merely about equipping individuals for piety but about enabling them to engage with their godlikeness, living purposefully in this life. This is not the distorted prosperity gospel aimed at exploiting believers but an effort to empower people with a fuller understanding of God's purpose.

Faith leaders often struggle with the idea of God working outside their defined boundaries. But as this work will continually stress, divine action is not confined to religious rituals. It is evident in innovations that serve humanity and advance God's kingdom. Consider the scientist who, though perhaps never attending church, works tirelessly to find a cure for cancer. Such efforts are driven not by guaranteed success but by faith in the capacity God has endowed humanity with—a faith that sees solving big problems as an expression of being made in God's image.

God has given us the gift of life and the hope to "give ourselves the gift of living well," as Voltaire once said. Faith, then, is not merely about adhering to religious norms but about trusting God's work through the capabilities He has placed within us. It is a faith that embraces both the spiritual and the practical, recognizing that innovation and service to humanity are as much acts of worship as any religious ritual.

Anointed for the Assignment, not the Commissioning

Back to the spies. While the Bible does not explicitly state that these spies were the same leaders anointed in Numbers 11, the evidence strongly suggests this connection. The Numbers 11 men were "the elders of Israel" (Numbers 11:16). The spies, too, were all "heads of the children of Israel" (Numbers 13:3). There is no reason to suggest that the ten spies who brought a bad report were low-level leaders. To be entrusted with a mission this critical to Israel's future, they were most likely among Moses' choice men and equal in stature and authority to Joshua and Caleb.

It's important to understand the criticality of faith and the prophetic in the story of Israel and its leadership. The Promised Land itself was grounded in a prophetic word. In Exodus 3:8, God told Moses of His plan to deliver the children of Israel from bondage and bring them to the land of Canaan. Moses relayed this promise to the people in Exodus 4, and it was this prophetic word that inspired their belief and their journey. The miracles they witnessed - from the plagues in Egypt to the parting of the Red Sea and the provision in the wilderness - were all the fulfillment of God's spoken promises.

Moses, often described as The Deliverer, is also recognized as a prophet. Deuteronomy 34:10 says, "No prophet ever rose again in Israel like Moses." His leadership was defined by the sure word of God, and Israel's leadership was meant to follow this pattern. Providing such leadership required faith, described in Hebrews 11:1 as "the substance of things hoped for, the evidence of things not seen." This faith was essential for Moses as he led the people based on God's promises rather than immediate challenges.

Moses' clear belief that anointing is for the assignment, not just for the commissioning, can be sensed in his response to Joshua when he sought to have Eldad and Medad silenced in Numbers 11:28: "Oh, that all the Lord's people were prophets and that the Lord would put His Spirit upon them!" Moses wished that everyone would hear clearly from God, that everyone would lead like he did - in faith and according to God's promise. Just as he emphasized to Joshua, Moses would have expected that the spies understood that faith counted in the assignments and that valuing and believing God's promises mattered in exercising the responsibilities that come with being chosen and called.

That was not the kind of leadership the ten spies brought to their assignment. Instead of seeing through the lens of God's promises as their leader Moses did, and which was God's expectation of those He called, chose, and anointed, they saw through the lens of fear. Because of their failure to carry faith and to value God's spoken word, they forfeited their ability to lead with vision and courage, leading to their faltering leadership.

The report they brought back seemed consistent with the instructions for their assignment in Numbers 13:17-20. Here is what they reported back:

"Now they departed and came back to Moses and Aaron and all the congregation of the children of Israel in the Wilderness of Paran, at Kadesh; they brought back word to them and to all the congregation, and showed them the fruit of the land. Then they told him, and said: 'We went to the land where you sent us. It truly flows with milk and honey, and this is its fruit. Nevertheless the people who dwell in the land are strong; the cities are fortified and very large; moreover we saw the descendants of Anak there. The Amalekites dwell in the land of the South; the Hittites, the Jebusites, and the Amorites dwell in the mountains; and the Canaanites dwell by the sea and along the banks of the Jordan.'"

The problem was not that they saw that the people of the land were strong, or that the cities were fortified, or that there were giants in the land. The problem was their conclusion about who they were based on what they saw, instead of how God saw them and what He had done. Their conclusion was that Israel was not capable of taking the land of promise. You can clearly see the hyperbole in their response to Caleb, who said the land could be taken, to justify their fears:

"The land through which we have gone as spies is a land that devours its inhabitants...and all the people whom we saw in it are men of great stature. There we saw the giants (the descendants of Anak came from the giants); and we were like grasshoppers in our own sight, and so we were in their sight."

In Chapter 2, we discussed the need for the faith community to be proactive and the importance of replacing unfounded fear with informed faith and engagement. True faith does not avoid knowing or seeing the challenges. It is precisely the kind of conclusions drawn by these spies that causes the faith community to withdraw from spheres of influence - technology, governance, science, and more - often to the detriment of godly principles because the challenges appear too great.

This assignment was not supposed to put fear in their hearts, but it did because they left their faith in Kadesh Barnea. It was why they saw themselves as grasshoppers and not as the godlike people equipped to take the land with God. They were supposed to lead God's people forward, doing life by faith. Instead, their report caused Israel to want to retreat.

The faith-filled perspective of Joshua and Caleb, who boldly proclaimed, "Let us go up at once and take possession, for we are well able to overcome it" (Numbers 13:30), rested on four truths:

1. **The promise was good:** "The land we passed through and explored is exceedingly good." (Numbers 14:7)
2. **Aligning their hearts with God's will was critical to securing it:** "If the Lord is pleased with us, he will lead us into that land, a land flowing with milk and honey, and will give it to us. Only do not rebel against the Lord." (Numbers 14:8-9)

3. **Courage was required to obtain God's promises:** "And do not be afraid of the people of the land, because we will devour them." (Numbers 14:9)
4. **God was present with them:** "Their protection has departed from them, and the Lord is with us. Do not fear them." (Numbers 14:9)

Joshua and Caleb understood that godlikeness—taking bold steps—must be accompanied by godliness, a heart aligned with God's will. The people did not want to hear this encouragement to reframe their perspective. They did not want any leader who urged them to press on, to go forward in faith. Those who did so risked being stoned. Instead, they demanded the type of leaders who would *"lead"* their retreat:

"So they said to one another, 'Let us select a leader and return to Egypt.'" (Numbers 14:4)

Fear Demands Wrong Leadership

When Israel's faith faltered, they cried out for leaders who would lead them back to Egypt. They said, "Let us select a leader and return to Egypt" (Numbers 14:4). This demand reflects a profound truth: fear often compels people to seek leadership that reinforces retreat rather than progress.

The leadership the children of Israel demanded after the bad report of the ten spies was not the type that would, by faith, lead in the direction of God's promise, but leadership that would lead in the direction of the people's desires. It would not be prophetic leadership led by God but leadership that was led by the people themselves, rooted in their own desires. This dangerous forgetfulness about past experiences—their miraculous deliverance from Egypt and God's provision along the way—led them to reject the very foundation of their journey. Instead of remembering God's faithfulness, they focused on their fears.

This tendency is not unique to ancient Israel. Today, the church often retreats from engaging with emerging technologies, forgetting the powerful liberating impact of past innovations like Gutenberg's printing press. This revolutionary technology made Scripture widely accessible, fostering literacy and empowering the Reformation. The gospel advanced as people became informed, not by retreating into safety but by engaging with the challenges of their time.

It is critical to remember that the gospel does not necessarily advance by avoiding challenges. Instead, it thrives when the faith community steps forward with informed faith, embracing both godlikeness and godliness. The Promised Land, which the Israelites finally entered, became the launching pad for the global Christian movement. Interestingly, this same land is now a hub of innovation, known as the start-up capital of the world. It is a powerful reminder that advancing into the unknown - guided by faith - creates spaces for God's purposes to unfold.

Kingdom leadership must guide in the direction of faith, grounded in God's promises and the courage to confront life's complexities. It must not be judged solely by its activity but by its alignment with God's will. Followers also play a critical role in demanding leadership that advances the Kingdom. By cultivating informed faith, believers can discern and support leaders who embody both godlikeness and godliness, ensuring that the community of faith continues to thrive and advance.

The Gift of Life as the Land of Promise

Two scriptures anchor our understanding of life and leadership: Genesis 1:26-28 and John 10:10. Genesis declares that we are created in God's image and given dominion, while John reveals Christ's purpose: "I have come that they may have life and have it to the full." These scriptures underscore that life itself is God's greatest gift, a promise to be lived abundantly in godlikeness and godliness.

1 Peter 3:7 calls us "heirs of the gracious gift of life." This gift of life, when lived fully in alignment with God's design, enables us to inherit the meta gift: "the gift of eternal life in Christ Jesus our Lord" (Romans 6:23). However, neglecting the present gift in pursuit of the eternal one diminishes both. A disengaged faith community that retreats from life's complexities and does not lend itself to solve them loses its witness.

We were not created simply to go to heaven; rather, we were created to live purposefully here on earth. Heaven is the reward for how we live this life, fully embodying the symbiosis of godlikeness and godliness. Consider Jesus' words in John

17:18: "As you sent me into the world, I have sent them into the world." Our purpose is to engage with and transform the world through the Spirit's empowerment.

The integration of godlikeness and godliness - dominion and alignment with God's will - is key to living abundantly. To neglect either is to diminish the life God has called us to lead. The gift of life is not just a temporal experience; it is preparation for eternity, where the fullness of God's promises is realized. By engaging fully with this life, we testify to the reality of the eternal one.

Spying Out the Future: Innovators and the Promise

Innovators today mirror the spies of Numbers 13, venturing into uncharted territory and discovering new possibilities. Secular innovators in fields like AI and biotechnology challenge the faith community to rediscover the courage of Joshua and Caleb. If those without a foundation of faith can achieve extraordinary breakthroughs, how much more should believers, equipped with God's promises, lead the way?

Fear, routine, and a lack of vision often hold faith communities back. But moving forward in the age of transformative innovations requires not just technical skill but renewed courage and faith.

Conclusion

Faith left behind is faith wasted. As Voltaire reminds us, "God gave us the gift of life; it is up to us to give ourselves the gift of living well." Living well means embracing both godlikeness and godliness as we navigate life. By doing so, we honor God's gift of life, becoming testimonies of His grace and power. By welcoming innovation as a divine tool, we expand our capacity to live abundantly and to advance the Kingdom in ways that glorify God. As we lead others, may we always move forward in faith, courageously advancing the Kingdom for God's glory.

Discussion Questions

1. Why do you think the ten spies in Numbers 13 saw themselves as grasshoppers, despite being chosen leaders?

2. How does the balance of godlikeness and godliness influence your approach to leadership?
3. In what ways can faith communities become centers of empowerment for holistic human agency?
4. How can innovation be viewed as an expression of godlikeness and godliness?
5. What role do followers play in shaping the direction of leadership within the faith community?
6. How can the church's history with technological revolutions like Gutenberg's printing press inform its approach to emerging technologies today?

Practical Exercises

1. **Perspective Reframing**: Reflect on an area in your life where fear has overtaken faith. Write down three faith-filled truths that counteract your fear and commit to acting on them.
2. **Faith Audit**: Assess your current involvement in activities that reflect godlikeness

and godliness. Identify one area where you can grow and take a tangible step this week.

3. **Empower Others**: Identify one person you lead or mentor. Encourage them with a faith-filled perspective on a challenge they are facing.

4. **Daily Prayer**: Dedicate a week to praying daily for the courage to lead forward, asking God for wisdom and strength to embody both godlikeness and godliness.

5. **Innovation Stewardship**: Explore an area of your life where innovation could enhance your ability to live abundantly. Identify one practical step to embrace that innovation and reflect on how it aligns with your faith.

6. **Historical Reflection**: Research how technological advances, like Gutenberg's printing press, impacted the spread of the gospel. Write about one way the church today can embrace innovation to advance God's Kingdom.

"Most of us have more potential than we will ever develop. What holds us back is often a lack of courage."

Gary Chapman

CHAPTER 7

Redeeming Innovation: Faith Beyond Fear

"I have become all things to all people
so that by all possible means I might save some.
I do all this for the sake of the gospel, that I may
share in its blessings."
1 Corinthians 9:22-23

Introduction

Faith and technology have often been viewed as conflicting forces, yet history reveals a different narrative - one where faith leaders have boldly embraced innovation to fulfill their divine calling. This chapter challenges the faith community to reframe its perception of technology, not as a threat but as a tool that can amplify God's purposes. From the Apostle Paul's use of papyrus to the Reformation's embrace of the printing press, this chapter explores how humanity's greatest need - to become fully alive in God's image - can be supported by technological advancements.

What is Humanity's Greatest Need?

Humanity was created in the image and likeness of God. The account in Genesis 2:7 tells us that God "breathed the breath of life" into man, and he became a living being. But the story takes a dramatic turn in Genesis 3 with the fall, which echoes across the ages through Paul's words in Romans 3:23: "For all have sinned and fall short of the glory of God." The New Century Version frames this as "falling short of God's glorious standard." This "glorious standard"- the capacity to live fully in alignment with God's intent - was inherent in the living being God created. Yet, sin introduced a rupture, leaving humanity diminished and perpetually falling short.

This universal sense of diminishment resonates deeply within us. It's why even the most capable among us often grapple with imposter syndrome, questioning our worthiness even in areas where we meet or exceed worldly standards. I believe humanity's greatest need is to become fully alive - to recover the wholeness of being that reflects the image of God. Yet, when this pursuit is divorced from godliness, it morphs into prideful ambition. At our core, there is a yearning to rise above the limitations of our humanity, a whisper that reminds us we were created not just as human beings but as reflections of divine godlikeness.

This is why, when God calls and empowers His children, He does so with the expectation that they will rise to meet His glorious standard. The words of Jeremiah 12:5 illustrate this vividly. After the prophet lamented the apparent futility of faith in a world where the wicked thrived, God's rebuke was pointed:

"If you have run with the footmen, and they have wearied you, then how can you contend with horses? And if in the land of peace, in which you trusted, they wearied you, then how will you do in the floodplain of the Jordan?"

God's response challenges Jeremiah - and us - to rise above the ordinary, to transcend our own limitations. He expected Jeremiah to contend with challenges far beyond what his humanity alone could endure: to run with horses and not falter, to face the floodwaters of life with unshakable faith. This divine expectation is not a burden but an invitation - an invitation to exceed the confines of our broken humanity and reclaim the godlikeness for which we were created.

At the heart of humanity's greatest need is the call to live fully, not as mere humans diminished by sin, but as beings restored and empowered to reflect the glory and purpose of God. This is the essence of true living, the fulfillment of our original design, and the antidote to the imposter syndrome that whispers of our inadequacy. To live up to God's standard is not to strive in vain but to embrace the divine capacity He has placed within us, transcending the fall and walking in the fullness of life He intended from the beginning.

Mankind Has God's Full Support to Obtain His Promises

God fully supports humanity's effort to live up to His calling, which is why 2 Peter 1:3 reminds us: "His divine power has given to us all things that pertain to life and godliness, through the knowledge of Him who called us by glory and virtue." For a clearer understanding, the New Century Version translates this as:

"Jesus has the power of God, by which he has given us everything we need to live and to serve God. We have these things because we know him. Jesus called us by his glory and goodness."

This verse emphasizes that everything we need to live and serve God - to meet His glorious standard - is already given to us. And how do we access these provisions? By knowing Him.

In this light, we should revisit Moses' lament in Numbers 11:29: "Oh, that all the Lord's people were prophets and that the Lord would put His Spirit upon them!" Moses wished for every Israelite to hear and know God for themselves, to be their own eyes and ears for divine guidance. Such a relationship with God would have equipped them to live fully and serve Him faithfully, avoiding the complaints and rebellion that often marked their journey to the Promised Land. Without this personal knowledge of God, they risked not only provoking His anger but also failing to receive His promises. As Joshua 5:6 recounts:

"For the children of Israel walked forty years in the wilderness, till all the people who were men of war, who came out of Egypt, were consumed, because they did not obey the voice of the Lord."

Gifts from Unexpected Sources

Ensuring that God's children access what He has provided often involves recognizing and leveraging gifts from unexpected sources. Ironically, history shows times when the church itself became an obstacle to God's broader plans, restricting access to what was meant to empower His people. This parallels Joshua's error in asking Moses to stop Eldad and Medad from prophesying outside the tabernacle. Like Joshua, the church has sometimes resisted efforts to democratize access to God's Word, preferring to maintain control through hierarchical structures.

The Reformation, which began in 1517, was a pivotal moment in this struggle. At its heart was the desire for individuals to access scripture and discover their godlikeness without the mediation of religious authorities. This movement was fueled by a revolutionary technological gift: Johann Gutenberg's invention of the printing press in 1440. The *Gutenberg Bible*, printed in the 1450s, marked the beginning of the age of printed books. Though devoutly Catholic, Gutenberg's innovation inadvertently became a cornerstone of the Protestant movement, enabling the mass production of religious texts. Martin Luther famously called Gutenberg's invention "God's highest and extremest act of grace."

Before the printing press, Bibles were laboriously copied by hand, controlled by the church, and accessible only to priests. Knowledge for the masses was filtered through clergy, heavily influenced by their interpretations. While the Catholic Church initially embraced the press as a *divine art* to *extend the glory of God,* it soon sought to use the technology to reinforce priestly authority rather than empower the laity. The church resisted translating the Bible into vernacular languages, calling it casting "pearls before swine." Gutenberg, however, believed the church's monopoly on scripture and such attitudes towards the laity grieved God. Though not a reformist, his invention fanned the flames of reform.

Communication Technology and the Pauline Epistles

Long before Gutenberg, another technological gift advanced God's kingdom: papyrus. The Apostle Paul, driven by the conviction that God's intent is for humanity to live fully and serve Him, leveraged papyrus to spread the gospel throughout the Roman Empire. Paul understood that personal knowledge of God empowers believers, releasing the divine potential within them: "for it is God who works in you to will and to act in order to fulfill his good purpose" (Philippians 2:13).

Paul's use of first-century communication tools and networks to share matters of faith, grace, and salvation was revolutionary. His letters, written on papyrus (derived from the pith of the papyrus plant) or parchment, in Koine Greek - the lingua franca of the time - were accessible across the Roman Empire. These writings allowed Paul to multiply his presence and push the gospel forward, even when he was physically absent.

Paul did not waste time debating whether papyrus was an appropriate medium because of its origins in Ancient Egypt, where it had been used for centuries to record pagan religious texts, government records, and literature. He recognized the neutrality of the tool and its potential to serve God's purposes. Even when imprisoned, Paul's faith pressed forward through his letters, ensuring the gospel reached places he could not.

Paul's approach to technology offers a vital lesson for today's faith community, particularly in an age dominated by innovations like artificial intelligence and virtual platforms. If Paul were alive today, he would not shy away from using modern tools - whether word processors, virtual preaching platforms, or AI tools like ChatGPT - to advance the gospel. Paul's strategy was always to maximize the resources available to him to serve the larger mission. As he wrote in Philippians 3:13-14:

"Brethren, I do not count myself to have apprehended; but one thing I do, forgetting those things which are behind and reaching forward to those things which are ahead, I press toward the goal for the prize of the upward call of God in Christ Jesus."

Modern technology offers the same opportunity for today's believers to reach forward. Virtual preaching, AI-driven tools, and digital platforms allow the Word of God to transcend geographical boundaries and reach audiences that physical presence could never achieve. Just as Paul entrusted his letters to messengers like Phoebe, Tychicus, and Onesimus, today's faith leaders can leverage technology to carry their messages into digital spaces.

James 2:18 reminds us: "Show me your faith without your works, and I will show you my faith by my works." Paul's works of faith included leveraging technology and innovation. He dictated his letters to amanuenses (scribes), as seen in

Romans 16:22 where Tertius identifies himself as the writer: "I, Tertius, who wrote down this letter, greet you in the Lord." Occasionally, Paul added a personal touch, as in Galatians 6:11: "See what large letters I use as I write to you with my own hand!"

Paul's letters were carried by trusted messengers and often read aloud to their recipients. Over time, these letters were copied, preserved, and shared widely, becoming foundational to Christian theology and practice. Modern technology -from live streaming sermons to AI-generated study aids - serves a similar purpose, amplifying the reach of the gospel.

The papyrus that facilitated the spread of Paul's letters was a gift from God, just as today's technologies are gifts. Thank God that Paul embraced these tools without fear or suspicion, recognizing their potential to advance the Kingdom. His willingness to innovate ensured a great harvest for the Kingdom, and his example challenges the faith community today to do the same - to leverage technology boldly in service of God's mission.

Experiencing the Promise

This chapter demonstrates that suspicion of technology based solely on its origins can be counterproductive. Innovations from unredeemed cultures have historically served humanity's highest needs. Papyrus, for example, was not just a useful tool but a revolutionary technology in the service of good. Similarly, Gutenberg's invention of the printing press - though created by a devout Catholic - became instrumental in the explosive growth of the Protestant movement. Without it, the Reformation might never have achieved its profound impact.

Compared to today's advancements, these earlier technologies moved at a pace that seems glacial. Yet, if the speed of modern technology makes it suspect, consider this: the people living under the protective shelter of Israel's Iron Dome would argue otherwise. The system's AI-driven ability to identify, detect, and intercept enemy missiles at lightning speed could, to borrow Martin Luther's description of the Gutenberg press, be seen as *God's highest and extremest act of grace.* Similarly, the rapid advancements in quantum computing have expedited research into cures for devastating diseases, transforming what once took decades into breakthroughs achieved in mere years.

Not all technologies are equal. Some do have the potential to cause tremendous harm - nuclear weapons being a prime example. Albert Einstein's famous lament captures this duality: "It has become appallingly obvious that our technology has exceeded our humanity." While this may apply to the destructive power of nuclear weapons, it is also true that the same nuclear fission and fusion processes have been harnessed for tremendous good. Nuclear energy has powered electricity grids, advanced scientific exploration, and driven innovations in transportation, such as powering ships and submarines. These applications illustrate the capacity of technology to serve both peace and human flourishing when wielded responsibly.

This book invites people of faith to move from the sidelines and experience the promise of these new technologies. Technological advancements have profoundly shaped my life, beginning with my first encounter with the Olivetti electric typewriter in 1985. This machine, equipped with lift-off correction tape, retired my portable manual typewriter soon after I arrived in the United States from Romania. Before this, I had written a 65-page thesis for my degree at the Ștefan Gheorghiu Academy using a manual typewriter, painstakingly producing three carbon copies with sheets of carbon paper sandwiched between. Corrections required white-out or a typewriter eraser, tools that now seem prehistoric. Even so, that manual typewriter was light years ahead of the technology available to the Apostle Paul and would have been an incredible upgrade for his amanuensis and reed pen.

I never cared who made the typewriter - only that it was better than anything I had used before. But less than a year and a half later, Apple released the Macintosh 128K and turned my world rightside up. If I had thought liftoff correction tape was impressive, the Mac's word-processing capabilities were revolutionary. With it and a dot matrix printer, I could edit and print polished papers that met the rigorous standards of professors like Ambassador Donald McHenry and Professor Madeleine Albright.

Technology empowered me to produce work that showed I belonged at Georgetown University's Edmund A. Walsh School of Foreign Service, where I was a Fulbright Scholar. It amplified my voice and allowed me to engage confidently with mentors like Henry Kissinger, Marvin Kalb, and John Finney, despite my humble beginnings as an African kid who once went to school barefoot and studied by candlelight.

This story speaks to the agnosticism of technology - its ability to empower anyone's journey, including yours. Imagine what you could achieve if you embraced and leveraged today's technologies to fulfill your highest calling.

Discussion Questions

1. What does it mean to live fully in the image and likeness of God? How can technology aid in this pursuit?
2. Reflect on the parallels between the printing press in the Reformation era and modern innovations like AI. How can faith communities leverage current technologies to fulfill God's purposes?
3. How do we balance embracing technology while remaining mindful of its ethical implications?

4. What lessons can we learn from Paul's approach to communication and technology that are applicable in today's context?

Practical Exercises

1. Identify a modern technology or tool that you have been hesitant to use. Research its potential benefits for advancing your personal or community mission.
2. As a group, brainstorm ways to use technology to address a specific challenge in your faith community, such as virtual outreach or digital discipleship.
3. Write a short reflection or prayer asking God to guide you in leveraging technology for His glory and purposes.
4. Create a plan to use a digital tool (e.g., social media, video conferencing, or AI tools) to share a message of faith with a broader audience.

"Once a new technology rolls over you, if you're not part of the steamroller, you're part of the road."

Stewart Brand - American Author/Entrepreneur

CHAPTER 8
Faith At the Speed of life

"When economies change,
family structures change."
Dr. Jawanza Kunjufu - Author

Introduction

Faith at the speed of life requires not only adapting to change but thriving amidst it. In a rapidly evolving world, where technology and societal shifts continuously redefine the landscape of work, education, and relationships, faith must remain steadfast yet agile. This chapter explores how timeless truths can intersect with modern realities to support families and empower communities. It challenges faith communities to provide resources, foster innovation, and restore the family unit as a cornerstone of society, even as economies and structures change.

Navigating Faith in Changing Times

Faith at the speed of life demands agility - the ability to integrate timeless truths with modern realities, empowering individuals and communities to thrive amid constant change. In our time, faith must navigate the reality articulated by Peter Drucker referenced earlier that "The only skill that will be important in the 21st century is the skill of learning new skills. Everything else will become obsolete over time." This underscores the need for adaptability in a world where rapid advancements continuously reshape the landscape of work, education, and life itself.

Faith must also address the reality noted by Dr. Jawanza Kunjufu, that "when economies change, family structures change." This truth highlights the profound impact of socio-economic shifts on the foundational unit of society: the family. Economic transformations - driven by technological innovation, globalization, or societal evolution - have redefined work, education, and relationships, often straining family cohesion.

Never before in human history have families faced such significant challenges to fulfilling Brad Henry's ideal: to be "the compass that guides us...

the inspiration to reach great heights, and our comfort when we occasionally falter." Faith communities are called to respond to these disruptions by offering support, resources, and teachings that uphold the family's divine mandate to multiply and fill the earth. By fostering strong, godly unions, they can help families navigate the complexities of modern life while remaining rooted in eternal truths.

The rapid pace of life in the 20th and 21st centuries has been driven by technological, economic, and cultural advancements. Many of these changes have positively impacted well-being. Urbanization introduced faster-paced lifestyles, competitive job markets, and efficient transit systems. Globalized economies and interconnected supply chains now demand swift responses to market changes and consumer expectations. Advances in information and communication technology (ICT) have facilitated instant communication, while innovations in transportation have reduced physical distances. Automation and artificial intelligence (AI) have increased productivity and set new standards for speed.

Yet not all impacts have been positive. Consumer culture fosters expectations of immediacy and instant gratification, while social media encourages shortened attention spans. These factors strain family relationships, leaving less time for meaningful connection. Faith communities, by embracing the tools of modernity while grounding members in godliness, can counteract these pressures and restore the family as a source of stability and nurture.

Restoring Families as a Witness to the World

Families are not only beneficiaries of technology; they are also key agents of cultural and spiritual transformation. By equipping families to thrive, the Church builds a foundation for broader societal impact.

Faith communities play a pivotal role in restoring families and empowering them to thrive in a world of rapid change. Thriving, faith-filled families are more than a source of stability - they are living testimonies of God's transformative power. Families grounded in love, unity, and godliness serve as tangible witnesses to the redemptive work of the gospel, offering hope to a broken world.

Leveraging technology to support family connection, education, and collaboration is essential. Tools like video conferencing platforms have become indispensable for virtual gatherings, even beyond the pandemic. AI-powered solutions, such as household management apps, provide untapped potential for simplifying daily life and fostering greater harmony. Faith communities must rise to the challenge of creating and participating in the development of such technologies, ensuring they meet the physical, emotional, and spiritual needs of families.

An example of this innovation is the **Kitchen Copilot app**, envisioned as part of our Kingdom work. In July 2024, our technology team, led by co-founder and CTO Scott Forsyth, delivered the first iteration of the app, which simplifies household management. Families can access over 200,000 recipes, plan meals tailored to dietary needs, and create shareable shopping lists. The app's AI-powered nutritional analysis system supports informed decision-making, while features like recipe sharing and cookbook creation preserve family culinary traditions for future generations.

By making kitchen management a joy rather than a burden, Kitchen Copilot fosters collaboration, reduces stress, and strengthens bonds of togetherness. Specialized features that assist with managing health conditions like diabetes empower caregivers and families to thrive, even amid life's challenges. This app is a testament to how faith-inspired innovation can address modern complexities while honoring the family's God-given role as the cornerstone of community.

Healthy families do more than support individual households—they reflect the redemptive power of the gospel to the broader world. Their joy, unity, and thriving relationships naturally draw the attention of neighbors, coworkers, and extended relations, sparking curiosity and creating opportunities to share the hope of faith.

Pioneering Innovations for Broader Impact

Faith communities have the unique potential to address systemic challenges that extend far beyond individual households. As explored in Chapter 3, issues like hyper-gentrification have reshaped neighborhoods and congregations, often leaving the faith community disengaged. However, collaborative faith-tech partnerships can empower disadvantaged communities with resources to navigate housing markets, combat predatory practices, and seize opportunities for homeownership.

This urgent need inspired the vision for *Truparity: The Equity Track*, a technology-powered social enterprise designed to bridge the knowledge and resource gaps that hinder disadvantaged individuals from integrating into transformed societies. I am challenging the faith community to partner in building this bold initiative, which will serve as the inaugural project on the challenge board of *The Issachar Coll3ctive*. *Truparity* aims to equip individuals and families with tools to thrive in a rapidly evolving world.

Launching simultaneously with the publication of this book, *The Issachar Coll3ctive* is a faith-driven innovation and impact platform that encourages collaboration among believers, technologists, and social impact leaders to tackle pressing global challenges. This transformative platform will focus on:

- **Regenerative Solutions**: Developing tools that renew and empower communities.
- **Broadening Knowledge**: Raising awareness of systemic challenges and opportunities.

- **Cross-Sector Partnerships**: Uniting stakeholders to maximize impact.
- **Timeless Approaches**: Creating sustainable solutions for enduring problems.

A centerpiece of *Truparity* is the AI-powered *Equity JROTC* program, which will equip public high school students from historically disadvantaged backgrounds with the education and resources needed to thrive in high-opportunity neighborhoods and cities. This initiative, modeled after the transformative impact of the Junior Reserve Officers' Training Corps (JROTC), will seek support from individuals passionate about social impact ventures, as well as from banks, realtors, philanthropists, and churches.

In alignment with the vision of this book, The Issachar Coll3ctive will also challenge wealthy individuals of faith to follow the example of former Google Chief Executive Eric Schmidt, who launched the $125 million AI2050 philanthropic project. Schmidt's initiative funds artificial intelligence research to solve "hard problems" in areas such as bias, harm, geopolitical conflict, and technological limitations. Similarly, The Issachar Coll3ctive will encourage believers to direct their resources toward innovative, Kingdom-focused solutions that address systemic challenges and amplify the Church's redemptive impact on society.

Through initiatives like *Truparity*, faith-driven social enterprises can meet families at their point of need, demonstrating how God's care extends to every aspect of life. By leading and implementing these solutions, the Church can restore families, strengthen communities, and magnify its witness, showcasing God's transformative power in a rapidly changing world.

Time and Chance in the Age of AI

Biblical imagery often reflects agrarian contexts, such as the parable of the sower. For modern audiences unfamiliar with sowing or reaping, these metaphors may seem distant. Yet, Ecclesiastes 9:11 resonates universally: "The race is not to the swift, nor the battle to the strong, nor bread to the wise, nor riches to the discerning, nor favor to the skillful; rather, time and chance happen to them all."

This scripture illustrates that life's outcomes are not solely determined by ability but also by timing and opportunity. In today's fast-moving world, opportunity windows vary dramatically. Unique skill sets may open broad windows when demand is high, while competitive environments demand immediate action.

Technology exemplifies this principle, democratizing opportunity and breaking down barriers:

- A small-town creator can sell products globally.
- Entrepreneurs can launch startups with minimal capital.
- Artists can monetize passions without gatekeepers.

This democratization aligns with humanity's divine design - created in God's image with inherent creativity and innovation. To seize these opportunities, believers need both vision and preparedness. Families, too, must adapt to this fast-moving reality by equipping themselves with tools and strategies that support their unique callings and strengthen their bonds.

Restoring and equipping families through technological innovation is not just a practical response to societal change - it is a spiritual mandate. By addressing the physical, spiritual, and emotional health of families, the Church positions itself as a transformative force, capable of bearing witness to God's unchanging love in a rapidly evolving world.

As we consider the role of technology in democratizing opportunities, it is crucial to recognize the responsibility to steward these gifts wisely. Mismanaging time and chance can lead to missed Kingdom opportunities, both for individuals and the Church.

The Worst Resources to Waste

The worst resources to waste in a time of unrelenting change are time and chance. In the age of AI and rapid technological disruption, the truth of Ecclesiastes 9:11 has never been more evident. The convergence of opportunity and preparedness becomes the catalyst for meaningful impact, yet the mismanagement of either can lead to irrelevance or missed potential.

Time, unlike material resources, is irretrievable. In a world of accelerating innovation, failure to act decisively can mean missing critical windows of opportunity. Businesses, individuals, and faith communities must recognize that what is available today may not be tomorrow. Kodak's story, for example, underscores the consequences of delaying decisive action in the face of disruptive change. What might have been an opportunity to lead an industry became a moment of irreversible decline due to hesitation and misplaced priorities.

Chance, in the biblical sense, is not random but part of God's providential design. Opportunities often appear unexpectedly, but their value is realized only by those prepared to seize them. Consider Jesus' parable of the ten virgins (Matthew 25:1–13). Five were prepared for the bridegroom's arrival, while the others squandered their time and missed their chance to enter the wedding feast. This parable underscores the importance of readiness - not just for the Church's ultimate hope but for its mission in the here and now.

In the present age, the combination of time and chance is embodied in technology's ability to create unprecedented opportunities:

- Time is redefined by tools that automate tasks, enabling people to focus on higher pursuits.
- Chance is democratized through platforms that grant global access to markets, ideas, and relationships.

However, wasting these resources - by clinging to outdated paradigms or hesitating in the face of change - undermines the ability to reflect God's redemptive work in the world. For families, this might mean failing to embrace tools that could strengthen relationships or equip children for a future defined by AI and innovation. For faith communities, it could mean losing relevance in a world searching for hope and guidance amid rapid change.

Seizing Time and Chance

To waste neither time nor chance, believers must cultivate discernment, readiness, and boldness. Discernment ensures that fleeting opportunities align with God's purposes. Readiness equips individuals and communities to act when the moment arises. Boldness enables stepping into uncertainty, trusting God's provision and guidance.

Consider the Church's role in equipping families to make the most of time and chance:

- **Time**: Families must learn to steward their time wisely, using digital tools to enhance productivity and strengthen connections rather than allowing them to create distractions or division.

- **Chance**: Families should be taught to recognize opportunities for growth, service, and innovation, fostering a mindset that sees God's hand in every moment.

The faith community, too, must step into this proactive role by encouraging innovation and equipping members to seize opportunities for Kingdom impact. The mandate is clear: the Church must be a catalyst for transforming fleeting moments of chance into lasting legacies of faith, hope, and love.

In a world where technology is reshaping the rules of engagement, believers are called to steward time and chance as gifts from God - gifts that can build His Kingdom when used wisely or squandered when ignored. The hour is coming, and it is here: we must be ready.

Discussion Questions

On Faith and Families in a Changing World

1. Dr. Jawanza Kunjufu notes that "when economies change, family structures change." How have economic and technological

changes shaped your family or faith community, for better or worse?

2. Reflecting on the tension between "godliness" (moral character) and "godlikeness" (creativity and purpose), how can families embody both in their daily lives?

3. How can faith communities provide practical tools and spiritual guidance to help families navigate the challenges of modern life?

On Faith-Driven Innovation

4. The Kitchen Copilot app is highlighted as an example of faith-inspired innovation. What other opportunities exist for faith communities to leverage technology for family or community well-being?

5. The chapter describes Truparity as a faith-driven initiative to address systemic challenges. How can your faith community support or replicate such a project to create meaningful impact?

6. How does restoring healthy, thriving families amplify the Church's witness to the world?

On Time and Opportunity

7. Ecclesiastes 9:11 reminds us that outcomes often depend on time and chance. How can families and faith communities prepare themselves to act when opportunities arise?
8. The parable of the ten virgins (Matthew 25:1–13) illustrates the importance of readiness. How can believers cultivate readiness in a world of rapid change?
9. How can the democratization of technology, which opens global opportunities, reflect humanity's God-given creativity and responsibility?

Practical Exercises

Personal Reflection

1. **Balancing Godliness and Godlikeness**
   Reflect on areas of your life where moral character and creativity feel out of balance. Write down one actionable step to bring greater harmony between these two aspects.
2. **Faith at the Speed of Life Audit**
   Identify one area of your family life strained by the pace of modern life. Brainstorm one

practical change—using technology or other means—that could alleviate this strain while fostering deeper connection.

Group Activities

3. **Innovation for Families Workshop**
Work in small groups to design tools or initiatives that strengthen family connections (e.g., shared calendars, storytelling platforms, or financial literacy tools). Present your ideas and discuss how they align with biblical principles of love and stewardship.

4. **Vision Casting for Truparity**
Collaboratively envision how Truparity or a similar initiative could be implemented in your community. Identify one specific issue (e.g., housing, education, or employment) and propose steps to address it through faith-driven innovation.

Strategic Planning

5. **Tech for Families Plan**
Develop a strategy for your faith community to educate families on using technology ethically and effectively. Include practical

examples like AI tools for meal planning, financial literacy, or caregiving.

6. **Legacy Redefined**

Reflect on Proverbs 13:22 ("A good man leaves an inheritance for his children's children"). Write down three ways your family or faith community can leave a legacy—spiritual, relational, or financial—that aligns with this verse.

Creative Engagement

7. **Building a Testimony through Innovation**

Write a short story or testimony about a family transformed by faith-driven technology (e.g., Kitchen Copilot or Truparity). Share it with your group or faith community to inspire further discussion and ideas.

8. **Faith and Technology Awareness Campaign**

Plan a campaign to educate your community about the potential of technology to strengthen families and advance the Kingdom. Include practical action steps and examples of faith-driven innovation.

Skills and Tools for the Future

9. **Family Innovation Toolkit**

   Create a "Family Toolkit" with recommended apps (e.g., budgeting, education, or meal planning tools) and spiritual practices (e.g., devotionals or prayer guides). Share this resource within your faith community.

10. **Opportunity Windows Role-Play**

    Role-play scenarios where families face sudden opportunities or challenges (e.g., a new tech tool or job relocation). Discuss how faith, preparation, and discernment can guide decision-making in such situations.

"Transformational leaders don't start by denying the world around them. Instead they describe a future they'd like to create."

Seth Godin - American Author/Entrepreneur

CHAPTER 9

Beyond "Amen": A Roadmap for Engaging Technology

"I slept and dreamt that life was joy.
I awoke and saw that life was service.
I acted and behold, service was joy."
Rabindranath Tagore - Indian poet and philosopher

Introduction

The Age of AI and emerging technologies presents unprecedented challenges and opportunities for the faith community. This dynamic landscape invites the faith community to act as both a moral compass and a catalyst for transformation, navigating these complexities with wisdom and vision. Yet, these opportunities are not self-executing. Without intentional engagement, the Church risks being sidelined in the very conversations that define the future of humanity. As American author M. Scott Peck reminds us, "the life of wisdom must be a life of contemplation combined with action." For the faith community, this means that the conclusion of prayer - the utterance of "Amen"- must mark the beginning of actionable engagement with the world.

Prayer and worship provide the spiritual foundation for action, but the light of faith is not meant to remain confined within the walls of the sanctuary. Like a candle lighting other candles, the faith community's mission is to extend its influence into every sphere of life. This chapter provides a practical roadmap for bridging the gap between theological reflection and actionable steps in engaging technology, guiding faith communities, leaders, and individuals to move beyond ritual into transformative impact.

1. Reclaiming the Historical Mandate of the Faith Community

Throughout history, the Church has been a leader in innovation and social impact. The establishment of the first hospitals was rooted in early Christians' belief in the sanctity of life. For example, in the United States, the three oldest hospitals - Pennsylvania Hospital, New York–Presbyterian Hospital, and Massachusetts General Hospital -

were all started by Christians motivated by charity and care for the poor. These institutions, originally designed to serve the underprivileged, became the foundation of modern medicine. Similarly, Christian universities such as Harvard, Oxford, and Yale were founded to advance knowledge in alignment with divine principles.

In recent times, the Church has continued to embrace technology. A few decades ago, it was unimaginable that multiple screens would guide worship or that apps like YouVersion could make the Bible accessible in over 20 versions on smartphones. A friend's son, hired as YouVersion's first Director of Marketing, expanded its reach from 300 million to 800 million downloads over seven years. This success demonstrates the power of faith-driven technological initiatives.

The question now is, what will be commonplace five years from now? While some express trepidation about pastors using AI to assist with sermon writing - including those who rely on others to plan sermons or employ ghostwriters for books - such discussions are not new. In Chapter 7, we examined Paul's use of amanuenses (scribes) to write his epistles, noting Tertius' acknowledgment in Romans 16:22: "I, Tertius, who wrote down this letter, greet you in the Lord." Though we cannot know how much Tertius may have influenced Paul's thoughts, it is clear that leveraging available resources - whether human or technological - has been a part of ministry since biblical times.

As we consider whether holograms or even robots might one day deliver sermons, these possibilities compel us to explore the potential of technology while remaining anchored in theological discernment. Moving beyond "Amen" means translating our spiritual convictions into active leadership in shaping the future.

Action Steps:
1. **Research and Celebrate Past Contributions:** Create resources that educate faith communities about their history of innovation to inspire confidence in their ability to lead.
2. **Launch Faith-Tech Hubs:** Establish innovation centers within churches or Christian organizations to explore and develop tech-based solutions to community challenges.

2. Applying the Archimedes Principle to the Work of the Faith Community

It is ironic that a famous saying attributed to the Chinese philosopher Lao Tzu, who is believed to have lived in the 6th century BCE, has only recently been embraced by the faith community as a critique of ineffective charity: "Give a man a fish, and you feed him for a day. Teach a man to fish, and you feed him for a lifetime." This proverb's recent adoption by faith organizations underscores two truths: the timelessness of wisdom and the tendency of the faith community to be late in recognizing it. This delay is a recurring challenge, but technology offers an unparalleled opportunity for the Church to catch up and implement programs with transformative impact.

A critical starting point is applying the Archimedes Principle to the faith community's missional work. Archimedes, the renowned mathematician and inventor of ancient Greece (born c. 287 BCE), famously declared: "Give me a lever long enough and a fulcrum on which to place it, and I shall move the world." This principle of leverage - the magnification of effort through the effective application of tools - is not confined to the mechanical world. It extends to the digital age, offering the Church the opportunity to amplify its reach and impact.

Moving beyond "Amen" requires bold action. The "long lever" of technology is as available to the faith community as it is to anyone else. By strategically positioning itself and utilizing the right technologies, the Church can transform aspirational goals into remarkable realities. Whether through digital platforms for education, AI tools for outreach, or blockchain for transparent resource management, technology can, with prayer and worship providing the spiritual "fulcrum," serve as the lever for impactful change moving the world forward.

Action Steps:

1. **Conduct a Technology Audit:** Assess existing tools and resources within faith communities to identify gaps and opportunities for leveraging technology effectively in mission work.

2. **Establish a Faith-Tech Task Force:** Form a dedicated team of tech-savvy individuals and community leaders to evaluate emerg-

ing technologies, recommend actionable initiatives, and guide the implementation of impactful solutions.

3. Building Multi-Stakeholder Partnerships

Moving beyond "Amen" means engaging with the broader world to create systemic change. By stepping out of the sanctuary and into the marketplace of ideas, the Church can ensure its light shines far and wide. Collaboration is critical to addressing the complex challenges of the modern world. Komborero Choga, a global leader in international development who has worked with UNICEF, Save the Children, World Vision International, and Compassion International across 55 countries, believes technology can drive significant efficiency and impact in humanitarian work. He emphasizes the importance of developing multi-stakeholder partnerships between faith communities, technology companies, and development organizations to create sustainable solutions. Choga envisions prioritizing the empowering of communities through knowledge transfer and capacity building over direct aid, leveraging technology for education, economic inclusion, improved access to medical care and resources, and developing platforms to connect marginalized individuals with vocational training and economic opportunities.

Action Steps:

1. **Convene Faith-Tech Forums:** Host events where faith leaders and tech innovators can network and explore collaborative opportunities.
2. **Pursue Joint Projects:** Identify areas where partnerships can address systemic issues, such as housing or digital literacy.

4. Empowering Communities Through Technology

Moving beyond "Amen" means empowering others to shine their light by providing them with tools and knowledge to put their faith into action. The faith community's role extends beyond advocacy or forming partnerships; it includes actively equipping individuals and communities to use technology in ways that enhance their spiritual, social, and economic well-being, all while upholding ethical standards. For example, digital literacy initiatives can bridge gaps for underserved communities by teaching them how to utilize technology for education, career growth, and civic participation. Additionally, faith-based organizations can develop applications that integrate spiritual resources, such as Bible translations and prayer guides, with practical tools like financial planning and health management aids, fostering a holistic approach to empowerment.

Action Steps:

1. **Launch Digital Literacy Campaigns:** Offer workshops and resources to help individuals and families navigate the digital world.
2. **Develop Faith-Centric Apps and Tools:** Create platforms that meet the spiritual and practical needs of communities while adhering to ethical standards.

5. Addressing Emerging Ethical Dilemmas

As technology evolves, it raises profound ethical questions that the faith community cannot ignore. From privacy concerns to the ethical use of AI in warfare, these issues demand thoughtful and biblically grounded responses. Moving beyond "Amen" requires engaging with these questions in the public square, offering a faith-informed perspective.

The Bible provides examples of people of faith courageously engaging in the public square to address ethical and moral challenges. One notable instance is the prophet Daniel, who served as an advisor to Babylonian and Persian kings while staying true to his faith. Despite living in a culture that often conflicted with his beliefs, Daniel used his God-given wisdom to navigate ethical dilemmas, from interpreting dreams to managing the affairs of the kingdom. His commitment to integrity and reliance on divine guidance made him a trusted voice in a secular environment, demonstrating how people of faith can contribute to societal decision-making without compromising their principles.

Today, the faith community can draw inspiration from such examples to address the ethical implications of emerging technologies. By participating in discussions on privacy, fairness, and the responsible use of AI, Christians can provide a moral framework grounded in justice, stewardship, and human dignity.

Action Steps:

1. **Establish Ethical Advisory Panels:** Form committees within faith communities to study and address emerging ethical dilemmas.

2. **Engage in Public Discourse:** Participate in broader societal conversations about the ethical use of technology, offering a faith-informed perspective.

6. Preparing for the Next Frontier

The faith community must not only respond to existing technologies but also anticipate what lies ahead. This requires a mindset of curiosity, adaptability, and readiness to engage with the unknown. By fostering a culture of innovation, the Church can ensure it remains a leader in shaping the future.

Biblical history provides inspiring examples of those who anticipated and prepared for future challenges with faith and vision. One such example is Joseph, whose interpretation of Pharaoh's dreams enabled Egypt to prepare for seven years of famine. His strategic foresight not only saved countless lives but also positioned him as a leader whose faith informed his practical decisions. Joseph's story demonstrates how faith can guide innovation and preparedness to meet both current and future needs.

In more recent times, people of faith like George Washington Carver exemplify the integration of innovation and spirituality. Carver's groundbreaking agricultural research was rooted in his deep faith, which he described as a source of inspiration for his scientific discoveries. His ability to foresee and address challenges in agriculture and sustainability provides a powerful model for how the faith community can lead in addressing modern technological frontiers.

Preparing for the next frontier requires the Church to adopt a similar posture -combining faith with innovation to anticipate and shape the future.

Action Steps:

1. **Foster a Culture of Innovation:** Encourage creativity and experimentation within faith communities to explore new technologies.

2. **Train Future Leaders:** Equip young believers with the skills and vision to lead in tech-driven industries, ensuring a legacy of faith-informed innovation.

Conclusion: Leading with Faith and Vision

The Age of AI challenges the faith community to move beyond fear and reactionary responses. By reclaiming its historical role as a leader in innovation, building partnerships, empowering communities, addressing ethical dilemmas, and preparing for the next frontier, the Church can ensure that technology serves humanity and glorifies God.

Beyond "Amen" lies the challenge and privilege of shaping the world for God's glory. As faith communities, we are called to illuminate the darkest corners of society, embracing technology not as a replacement for faith but as a tool to bring faith into action. The choices we make today will shape the world of tomorrow. As we stand at this pivotal moment, let us rise to the occasion with faith, creativity, and courage, knowing that the God who called us to be stewards of creation also equips us to meet the challenges of our time.

Discussion Questions

1. **Reclaiming the Historical Mandate**
   - How can the Church draw inspiration from its historical contributions to innovation, such as the establishment of hospitals and universities, to address modern challenges?
   - What lessons can be learned from successful faith-driven technological initiatives like YouVersion for future projects?

2. **Building Multi-Stakeholder Partnerships**
   - How can faith communities effectively partner with technology companies and international development organizations to address global issues like poverty and education inequality?
   - What role can faith leaders play in creating and sustaining partnerships that leverage technology for societal impact?

3. **Empowering Communities Through Technology**
   - What are some practical ways faith communities can address the digital divide and ensure equitable access to technology for marginalized populations?

- How can churches balance the integration of technology with the preservation of spiritual authenticity and community connection?

4. **Addressing Emerging Ethical Dilemmas**
   - What ethical challenges posed by AI and emerging technologies should the Church prioritize, and why?
   - How can theological principles such as stewardship and justice guide the faith community in addressing issues like privacy and the use of AI in decision-making?

5. **Preparing for the Next Frontier**
   - What innovations or trends do you foresee having the most significant impact on the Church in the next decade?
   - How can the faith community cultivate a culture of innovation while maintaining its core mission and values?
   - How do examples like Joseph and George Washington Carver inspire practical strategies for the faith community to lead in future technologies?

Practical Exercises

1. **Research and Reflection**
   - Research one historical example of a faith-driven innovation (e.g., the founding of a hospital or university) and write a short reflection on how its principles can be applied to modern technological challenges.

2. **Tech Literacy Workshops**
   - Organize or participate in a workshop designed to teach digital literacy or AI basics to members of your community. Document insights or feedback gathered during the session.

3. **Ethical Framework Development**
   - Form a small group to draft a framework that outlines ethical considerations for using AI in ministry or community work. Present the framework to your faith community for discussion and feedback.

4. **Create a Faith-Tech Vision Statement**
   - Develop a personal or organizational vision statement for how your church or faith-based organization could leverage technology to address one of the

five global philanthropic focus areas. Include specific technologies and steps to implement the vision.

5. **Foster Innovation Challenges**
    ○ Host an innovation challenge within your faith community where members propose tech-based solutions to real-world problems (e.g., poverty alleviation, education, or healthcare). Offer mentorship and recognition for the best ideas.

6. **Engage in Public Discourse**
    ○ Write an op-ed or blog post about a pressing ethical dilemma in technology, providing a faith-informed perspective. Share it with your community or submit it to a local publication.

7. **Develop a Digital Strategy**
    ○ Collaborate with other members of your faith community to create a strategic plan for integrating technology into one area of ministry, such as outreach, education, or worship.

"Before the foundation of the
earth was, the Lamb was slain."
Revelation 13:8

CHAPTER 10
It's Coming. It's Here.

"But the hour is coming, and now is, when
the true worshipers will worship
the Father in spirit and truth; for the
Father is seeking such to worship Him."
John 4:23-24

Introduction

Jesus' declaration to the Samaritan woman at the well captures the paradox of a present-future reality. The hour is both coming and now is. This is not merely a theological statement but an urgent call to live in the tension between what is anticipated and what is already here. It invites believers to engage with the present as if the future has already broken into it.

Yet, the faith community often fails to embody this urgency. While we profess anticipation of God's Kingdom, we remain rooted in the past, clinging to traditions and structures that hinder our ability to respond to present realities. Meanwhile, the Sundars of our age—innovators and technologists—relentlessly bring the future into the now, reshaping the world with artificial intelligence, renewable energy, and space exploration. Their actions demand a response from the faith community: Will we engage with the present-future reality or remain stuck in the past?

The Cost of Living in the Past

History offers sobering lessons for those who fail to adapt to the present-future reality. Businesses, institutions, and even entire industries that resisted change have faced devastating consequences. One stark example is the failure of many brick-and-mortar businesses to anticipate the shift to online shopping. These businesses insisted on defining themselves by outdated models, dismissing the headwinds of technological transformation driven by changing consumer preferences. Their resistance to change became their undoing.

Kodak, once an iconic American company, serves as another cautionary tale. In 2012, Kodak filed for bankruptcy, not because it ignored innovation entirely, but because it failed to fully embrace the disruptive forces shaping its industry. As Scott D. Anthony, a professor at Dartmouth College's Tuck School of Business, explains:

"Companies often see the disruptive forces affecting their industry. They frequently divert sufficient resources to participate in emerging markets. Their failure is usually an inability to truly embrace the new business models the disruptive change opens up. Kodak created a digital camera, invested in the technology, and even understood that photos would be shared online. Where they failed was in realizing that online photo sharing was the new business, not just a way to expand the printing business."

The lesson for faith communities and faith-based institutions is clear: having one foot in the past and another in the present-future is insufficient. Whether it is businesses or churches, resisting transformative trends will only lead to decline. If even the most well-resourced companies falter under the weight of partial adaptation, how much more should the faith community prepare to engage with the present-future reality wholeheartedly?

God and the Future

Albert Einstein once remarked that "the distinction between past, present, and future is only a stubbornly persistent illusion," a statement rooted in his scientific approach and methodology. Revelation 13:8 tells us that the Lamb was slain before the foundation of the earth, suggesting the non-linearity of Kingdom timelines. According to Acts 17:28, we "live, move, and have our being" in God, who is both the Alpha and the Omega, the beginning and the end (Revelation 22:13). For God, who transcends time, the past, present, and future are not separated by rigid boundaries but are instead facets of His eternal nature. In Him, these dimensions converge, allowing us the possibility of experiencing them within Him.

1. **The Presence of God as the Presence of the Future**

   God's presence is not merely about comfort or guidance in the now; it is the breaking-in of His eternal future into the present. In His presence, the reality of the Kingdom of God - the future renewal of all things - is experienced here and now.

- Isaiah 65:17: God proclaims, "Behold, I will create new heavens and a new earth." This prophetic vision of the future becomes tangible whenever God's presence manifests, signaling the foretaste of this renewal.
- Revelation 21:3-4: "Now the dwelling of God is with men, and he will live with them." God's ultimate purpose is to dwell with His people in fullness, and His presence in the present is a down payment of this future.

2. **The Overlap of the Present and the Future**

   The Bible reveals a tension between the "already" and the "not yet" of God's Kingdom. Through His Spirit, God's future reality invades the present, empowering His people to live as if the future is already here.

   - Luke 17:20-21: Jesus declares, "The kingdom of God is in your midst." The presence of Jesus is the presence of the future Kingdom breaking into the present world.
   - Acts 2:17: Quoting Joel, Peter says, "In the last days, God says, I will pour out

my Spirit on all people." The Spirit's presence marks the inbreaking of God's future into human history.

God's presence is a signpost of the world to come, where His will is done "on earth as it is in heaven" (Matthew 6:10). This reality urges us to act with Kingdom values now.

3. **Rituals Without God Obscure the Future**
   Rituals, when rightly oriented, point to God and His future promises. However, when they replace God's presence, they obscure the vision of the future and paralyze the community.

   ○ **Isaiah 1:11-17**: God critiques empty rituals disconnected from justice and mercy. They represent a faith disconnected from God's active presence and future.

   ○ **Matthew 23:23**: Jesus rebukes the Pharisees for prioritizing rituals over "justice, mercy, and faithfulness." Their focus on the present form blinded them to the transformative power of the future.

   Faith communities that prioritize rituals over God's presence stagnate, failing to embody the urgency of the present-future reality.

4. **If the Faith Community is Not Innovating, Is God Present?**

Consider the example of Peter walking on water in Matthew 14:28-31. Peter steps out of the boat because Jesus - the presence of God - is there, embodying the future reality of faith and possibility. His ability to innovate -to do something unprecedented - is directly tied to God's presence.

This raises a critical question: *If the faith community is not innovating, is God present?* If God's presence is the presence of the future, then His people should reflect this by boldly stepping into new realms of creativity, justice, and mission. Without this, we risk becoming like Peter when he doubted and began to sink - disconnected from the reality of God's power and future.

5. **Urgency in Action**

The present-future reality calls for urgency. To live as true worshippers is to embrace life's challenges and opportunities as arenas for worship. This requires:

- **Bold Engagement**: Addressing unredeemed spaces with creativity and courage. Like Peter stepping out of the boat, faith requires bold action.
- **Redemptive Innovation**: Leveraging technology and resources to confront injustice and brokenness. The faith community must reflect the future Kingdom by solving real-world problems.
- **Holistic Flourishing**: Thriving in every aspect of life as a testimony to God's glory. True worship brings transformation to individuals, families, and communities.

6. **Living in the Reality of the Present-Future**

Faith communities are called to live in the tension of the "already" and "not yet." God's presence assures us that the future has begun, and we are to live in its reality.

- **Philippians 3:20-21**: "But our citizenship is in heaven, and we eagerly await a Savior from there." Living as citizens of God's future Kingdom shapes how we act in the present.

○ **Matthew 28:20**: Jesus' promise, "I am with you always," connects His presence with the ongoing mission of His followers. It is the presence of the future that empowers their actions.

This urgency aligns with the call to act now, as God's people anticipate the culmination of His Kingdom while living in its present reality.

Living in the Present-Future

True worship, as Jesus describes, is not confined to rituals or locations but encompasses every aspect of life. Worship in spirit and truth calls believers to:

1. **Worship in Spirit**: Engage dynamically with God's presence, reflecting His creativity and compassion in our actions. Like Joseph in Egypt, whose strategic wisdom preserved a nation, our lives become worship when aligned with God's purposes.

2. **Worship in Truth**: Live out our godlikeness, our identity as God's image-bearers, embracing innovation and creativity as acts of worship. This truth extends beyond in-

tegrity to reflect God's character in transformative ways.

The fundamental leadership task explained in
Quantum Leadership is how we as people of faith
and disciples of Christ should live:

"Imagine not just learning to live within the
context of a whole new set of emergent conditions but leading others to embrace these shifts in
their own lives. This is the fundamental leadership
task – dealing with the same changes as everyone
while helping others thrive in a new reality."

Conclusion: Worship That Transforms

The hour is not just coming; it is here. God's
presence is the presence of the future, breaking
into the present and calling us to bold, transformative action. Let us reject hollow rituals and
embrace the reality of worship in spirit and truth.
By living as agents of God's future, we bring His
Kingdom to bear on the present, transforming
the world and embodying the hope of what is to
come.

Discussion Questions

On the Present-Future Reality

1. How does Jesus' statement in John 4:23-24 about "true worshippers" reflect the tension between the present and future realities of God's Kingdom?

2. In what ways can faith communities embody the "already" and "not yet" of God's Kingdom in today's world?

3. How does the story of Kodak illustrate the dangers of partially embracing change, and how does this reflect the wisdom of Proverbs 22:3, where the prudent prepare but the simple suffer?

4. What does it mean for faith communities to have both feet firmly in the present-future, as demonstrated by Peter stepping out of the boat in Matthew 14:28-31?

5. What are some examples of how the presence of God acts as a foretaste of the future renewal of all things, as seen in Isaiah 65:17 and Revelation 21:3-4?

On Rituals and Presence

6. How can rituals, when disconnected from God's presence, obscure the vision of the future, as critiqued in Isaiah 1:11-17?

7. How does Matthew 23:23 rebuke prioritizing rituals over "justice, mercy, and faithfulness," and how might this apply to modern faith practices?

8. How can faith communities ensure their rituals remain connected to God's active presence and point toward His future promises, as seen in Luke 17:20-21?

On Innovation and Faith

9. If God's presence is the presence of the future, what role should innovation play in the life of faith communities, in light of the lessons from Acts 2:17?

10. How can bold engagement, redemptive innovation, and holistic flourishing reflect the reality of God's Kingdom in the present, as called for in Matthew 6:10?

11. How can the faith community ensure it is not merely accommodating change but

leading transformation, as Ezekiel 33:6 urges watchmen to do?

12. What are some examples of how clinging to old paradigms has hindered faith-based organizations, and how might Isaiah 43:19 challenge us to "see" the new things God is doing?

13. How might the Church redefine its identity and mission to better reflect the realities of a rapidly changing world, as Philippians 3:20-21 reminds us of our heavenly citizenship?

On Worship in Spirit and Truth

14. What does it mean to worship in spirit and truth, as described by Jesus in John 4:23-24?

15. How can worship be expressed through creativity, innovation, and solving real-world problems, reflecting God's character as Creator (Genesis 1:27)?

16. What might living as "citizens of God's future Kingdom" look like in your personal or community life, as encouraged by Matthew 28:20 and Philippians 3:20-21?

Practical Exercises

Personal Reflection

1. **Mindset Shift**
   Reflect on an area of your personal or spiritual life where you might be straddling the past and the present-future. Consider how Philippians 3:20-21, which reminds us of our heavenly citizenship, can inspire you to fully embrace the future.

2. **Living the Present-Future**
   Write down examples of how you see God's future Kingdom breaking into the present in your life or community. Reflect on how this aligns with Jesus' prayer in Matthew 6:10, "Your kingdom come, Your will be done, on earth as it is in heaven."

Group Activities

3. **Case Study: Kodak and Beyond**
   - Research the story of Kodak or another company that failed to adapt (e.g., Blockbuster, Toys "R" Us).
   - Discuss parallels between their failures and challenges faced by faith communi-

ties today, using Proverbs 22:3 as a guide for proactive preparedness.

4. **Present-Future Strategy**
   - Identify one area in your faith community that is rooted in outdated models.
   - Develop a plan to reimagine it in light of Isaiah 43:19: "See, I am doing a new thing! Now it springs up; do you not perceive it?"

The Futureproofer's Grace

With hands that weave the
threads of time,
She plans ahead, her vision sublime.
A master of life, resourceful and wise,
Her faith and foresight help her rise.
She laughs at the days yet to unfold,
Her strength and wisdom
more precious than gold.
Anchored in purpose,
she charts her way,
The Proverbs 31 woman
futureproofs each day.

Noah Manyika - 2025

CHAPTER 11
Futureproofing

"Go to the ant, you sluggard!
Consider her ways and be wise, Which, having no
captain, Overseer or ruler, provides her supplies
in the summer, and gathers
her food in the harvest."
Proverbs 6:6-8

Introduction: The Call to Reflect and Prepare

At this pivotal point in the book, I invite you to pause and reflect on why this message matters and why you should continue reading. This chapter serves as a bridge to vital discussions ahead, including:

- The Theology of Giftedness
- The Symbiosis of Godlikeness and Godliness
- The Habits of Godlikeness and Godliness

In my view, fulfilling humanity's defining quest and divine calling in the most God-honoring way requires theological grounding. We are a complete work, fearfully and wonderfully made (Psalm 139:14), designed to thrive in both life and godliness. This involves understanding that God's plan for human redemption is not partial - meant only to liberate us for godliness while leaving our godlikeness under the curse of the fall. It would be impossible for us to "**have life** and **have it more abundantly**" (John 10:10) if that were the case.

In Acts 17:26–27, Paul says: "And He has made from one blood every nation of men to dwell on all the face of the earth, and has determined their preappointed times and the boundaries of their dwellings, so that they should seek the Lord, in the hope that they might grope for Him and find Him, though He is not far from each one of us."

The phrase "every nation of men being made from one blood" suggests that the rules of redemption apply to everyone, including the Sundars, the Nadellas, and the Huangs, who have risen from humble beginnings to helm today's tech giants. When Christ "led captivity captive and gave gifts to all men" (Ephesians 4:8), no one was left out. Notice, however, that the scripture does not say the gifts were given to those who believed. It simply states that He "gave gifts to men." This explains why "they" too can do extraordinary things - because "they" too were made in the image and likeness of God. We will discuss this further in the next chapter, but for now, let us focus on the subject of this chapter: Futureproofing.

What is Futureproofing?

Commonly, futureproofing refers to designing, building, or planning for resilience against potential challenges and disruptions. It involves anticipating trends, risks, and uncertainties and adapting strategies to maintain long-term relevance.

The biblical story of Joseph's work in Egypt, as recounted in Genesis 41, is a powerful example of futureproofing. After interpreting Pharaoh's dream about the impending famine, Joseph suggested that Egypt's ruler "select a discerning and wise man, and set him over the land of Egypt" to implement the futureproofing plan (Genesis 41:33–36). Pharaoh's response:

"And Pharaoh said to his servants, 'Can we find such a one as this, a man in whom is the Spirit of God?' Then Pharaoh said to Joseph, 'Inasmuch as God has shown you all this, there is no one as discerning and wise as you.'" (Genesis 41:38–39).

Joseph's qualifications as a futureproofer, as listed by Pharaoh, were:

1. A man in whom is the Spirit of God.
2. A man who could see the future.
3. A man who was discerning.
4. A man who was wise.

Reflect on these qualities, as they will resurface later in this chapter.

The Ultimate Act of Futureproofing

Let us consider futureproofing from a different perspective. What is the ultimate reason for preaching the gospel? The answer is simple: so that those who hear might be saved and receive eternal life.

In John 3, Jesus declares to Nicodemus: "And as Moses lifted up the serpent in the wilderness, even so must the Son of Man be lifted up, that whoever believes in Him should not perish but have eternal life." (John 3:14–15).

To accept Christ is to embrace the ultimate assurance of eternal life. Through belief in Him, we are guaranteed a future that transcends the uncertainties of this world. Being born again (John 3:3) is, therefore, the ultimate act of futureproofing - ensuring that regardless of earthly disruptions, eternal fellowship with God is secure.

As 1 Timothy 2:3-4 reminds us, however, God does not merely desire that we be saved but also that we "come to the knowledge of the truth." This knowledge empowers us to thrive in this life while securing eternal life. God's divine power has given us all we need for life and godliness (2 Peter 1:3), equipping us to live abundantly (John 10:10). While godliness pertains to the ultimate act of futureproofing (eternal life), tapping into our god-likeness enables us to futureproof in this life.

The Mathematics of Life: Lessons from Proverbs

The ability to see the future is a critical quality of a futureproofer. Proverbs 13:22 states: "A **good man** leaves **an inheritance** to his **children's children**."

This verse highlights two essential truths:
1. Good men understand the mathematics of life.
2. They futureproof their resources to overcome challenges ahead.

The Proverbs 31 woman, who clearly understood the mathematics of life, exemplifies this ability. The greatest vulnerability for people in the 21st century is being trained for careers but not for mastering life. Careers, and the skills we acquire to pursue them, often become obsolete over time. As management consultant Peter Drucker observes: "The only skill that will be important in the 21st century is the skill of learning new skills."

The Proverbs 31 woman offers a timeless blueprint for navigating life's complexities with resourcefulness, adaptability, and faith. This *Jill of many trades and master of life* understood that a single income stream was insufficient. Similarly, a man who leaves an inheritance to his children's children must be a *Jack of many trades and master of life.*

Had both lived in Charlotte, NC, today, they would understand that a million dollars is no longer what it was 15 years ago. A three-bedroom bungalow in Optimist Park, valued then at $85,000, might now sell for upwards of $500,000 with just $50,000 in improvements. However, they would also recognize the opportunities to make a million today that did not exist 15 years ago, leveraging the God-given capacity for reinvention.

The Challenge of a Changing World

Reid Hoffman's prediction, discussed in Chapter 2, that the traditional 9-to-5 workday may disappear by 2034, highlights the need for adaptability. It would be tempting for the faith community to respond to this prediction much like the people who saw Saul prophesying in 1 Samuel 10:11: "And it happened, when all who knew him formerly saw that he indeed prophesied among the prophets, that the people said to one another, 'What is this that has come upon the son of Kish? Is Saul also among the prophets?'"

Will Hoffman's prediction come true? Perhaps some might even point out that one of his recent predictions - that Kamala Harris would beat Donald Trump in the 2024 Presidential election - did not materialize.

Hoffman likely does not fancy himself a prophet. His prediction, not a prophecy, may overstate the idea that every 9-to-5 job will disappear. Whether or not his forecast fully materializes, the question remains:

Will your job exist in 2034?

For many, this question provokes fear. If the answer is "no," a cascade of concerns arises. You may still be in debt from an education that gave you qualifications for the only career you have spent much of your life preparing for. It's possible that the only thing you know how to do is what you are doing now. Perhaps you have a thirty-year mortgage on your home, 5-year car note, and have no savings. If you are in your thirties today, you will be in your forties then, pondering what the second half of your life will look like.

If you are the leader of a Bible school or seminary, the question also confronts you: How do you avoid going the way of the Christian bookstore which is the focus of the case study at the end of this chapter? How do you futureproof your mission? If you are a church or faith-driven organization - perhaps in a hyper-gentrifying city like Charlotte - how do you futureproof your Kingdom work from the existential challenges, changes, trends, or disruptions? How do you reconcile doing the eternal work of the church with temporal opportunities? How do you impart timeless values, ensuring they are deeply grounded, even as the places where you can physically reach people become harder to maintain?

Leveraging Technology and AI to Futureproof

It's important to think of AI not in isolation but as part of the broader opportunities presented by the Age of AI. Leveraging the opportunities of any age requires a certain type of mindset and self-awareness. Becoming a Joseph or a Proverbs 31 woman requires more than prayer; it demands action and preparation.

This message is not for those who use the Word of God to excuse laziness or who blame systemic injustices for all their struggles. While Joseph was falsely accused, he was practically a convicted felon who still developed the gifts that eventually brought him before Pharaoh. Are you working the gifts within you - those that can bring you into the presence of kings (Proverbs 18:16) and elevate you?

A tool is only as effective as the person wielding it. While AI or other technologies can empower your dreams, you must first have a dream. While these tools can help organize your thoughts, you must first think. While they can bring efficiencies to your work, expedite research, and aid in building projects, you must first be doing something.

It is ironic that the faith community often cries about being silenced in the public square while simultaneously rejecting tools that could amplify its voice. We decry systemic barriers to accessing information but feel overwhelmed in this era of democratized access.

In Chapter 3, we discussed Proverbs 15:14: "The heart of him who has understanding seeks knowledge, but the mouth of fools feeds on foolishness." We are compelled by the understanding that comes from redemption to pursue knowledge. However, we do not always feel compelled to act on this understanding. Others do - not because they understand redemption but because they understand the gift of being human.

The greatest opportunity in the Age of AI is not just to know but to know *how to*. Leaders like Sundar Pichai, Satya Nadella, and Jensen Huang ascend to the apex of their industries because their quest extends beyond acquiring knowledge to mastering its application.

The Proverbs 31 woman exemplifies this principle. She knew how to evaluate opportunities and invest wisely. She worked diligently with both her mind and her hands. She understood the value of time and service to others and engaged in commerce with skill and ingenuity. She was informed, spoke with wisdom, and faced the future with confidence, anchoring her preparation and ambitions in God's eternal purposes. This is how she futureproofed her life and that of her family.

Conclusion: Anchored in Him

The ultimate way to futureproof is by living out the reality of Acts 17:28:

"For in Him we live and move and have our being." In Him, godlikeness and godliness empower humanity to fulfill both the Creation Mandate and the Great Commission. As you reflect on this chapter, consider how God is calling you to prepare - not with fear, but with faith and boldness. Think of the qualities of a futureproofer as listed by Pharaoh and think of where you fall short and what you need to do to be

1. A man/woman in whom is the Spirit of God.
2. A man/woman who can see the future.
3. A man/woman who is discerning.
4. A man/woman who is wise.

The tools and principles discussed here are an invitation to step into the next chapter of your life, equipped to meet the challenges and opportunities of the Age of AI. Let courage and vision guide you forward. You will not find discussion questions or practical exercises at the end of this chapter. Instead, reflect its contents and the issues raised in the following case study as you prepare to dive into the second half of *Redeeming Sundar: Faith and Innovation in the Age of Ai.*

Case Study: The Demise of the Christian Bookstore Sector—A Failure to Futureproof

Introduction: A Once-Thriving Marketplace

For much of the 20th century, Christian bookstores were a pillar of faith-based commerce. These stores were not just retail spaces; they were cultural hubs, places of ministry, and vital community gathering spots for believers seeking books, music, gifts, and other resources that aligned with their faith. At their height, chains like

Family Christian Stores, LifeWay Christian Stores, and independent shops thrived in suburban shopping centers and downtown districts. They offered a unique value proposition: curated Christian content in a faith-centered environment.

However, by the late 2010s, this industry collapsed. Family Christian Stores, once the largest chain of Christian bookstores in the U.S., closed all 240 of its locations in 2017. LifeWay shuttered its brick-and-mortar stores in 2019, transitioning to a digital-only model. Hundreds of independent Christian bookstores followed suit, unable to keep up with changing consumer behavior and market dynamics.

The collapse of the Christian bookstore sector serves as a stark case study in the failure to future-proof—a failure that is particularly instructive because it was not just a business failure, but also a failure of vision, adaptation, and theological imagination in an era of digital transformation.

1. The Digital Disruption That Was Foreseen but Ignored

By the early 2000s, it was evident that retail was undergoing a seismic shift. Amazon, founded in 1994, had transformed book retail into an online-first business model. Meanwhile, digital e-books, audiobooks, and online Christian content platforms were gaining traction. The writing was on the wall: consumer habits were shifting rapidly toward e-commerce, and bookstores of all kinds - not just Christian ones - needed to innovate or risk obsolescence.

Secular bookstores faced similar headwinds but responded with varying degrees of adaptability. Barnes & Noble, while struggling, diversified its business through its Nook e-reader, in-store events, and partnerships. Independent bookstores leveraged community engagement, unique in-store experiences, and digital integration to survive. Christian bookstores, however, largely resisted these shifts.

The failure was not due to ignorance - these changes had been visible for over a decade before the collapse. More than two years before Family Christian Stores, which employed over 3,000 people, shut down, its suppliers had written off $127 million in debt to keep the chain afloat. According to a *Christianity Today* article published on February 23, 2017, when the company finally closed after 85 years in business, it cited "changing consumer behavior and declining sales" as the primary reasons.

What we see with Christian bookstore operators is a failure of decisive action. Many assumed their core audience would remain loyal regardless of broader market trends. This miscalculation proved fatal.

2. A Misplaced Trust in Community Loyalty

Christian bookstores often positioned themselves as more than just retail shops—they were ministries. This was a strength but also a weakness. Many owners and managers assumed that their faith-driven customer base would prioritize supporting Christian-owned businesses over the convenience of online shopping.

However, even the most faithful consumers operate within economic realities. Price sensitivity, convenience, and selection drive purchasing decisions across all demographics, including religious ones. Amazon and online retailers offered greater variety, competitive pricing, and the convenience of doorstep delivery. The assumption that loyalty would override these factors underestimated the power of market forces.

Meanwhile, Christian consumers, increasingly engaged in digital spaces, discovered that community could be fostered online just as effectively as in-store. Faith-based social media groups, Christian book clubs on platforms like Goodreads, and direct-to-consumer digital ministries rendered the in-store experience less necessary. By the time bookstore chains realized this, it was too late to pivot.

3. A Theology That Discouraged Innovation

Beyond business missteps, there was a deeper issue: a cultural and theological resistance to innovation. Many Christian bookstores were operated with an implicit belief that faith-based businesses should not operate under the same market-driven imperatives as secular ones. There was a prevailing sense that because these stores were engaged in ministry, they were somehow insulated from the disruptions affecting mainstream retail.

This mindset led to several miscalculations:

- **A reluctance to embrace digital transformation:** Many Christian bookstores delayed e-commerce integration, underinvested in digital content, and failed to build strong online communities.
- **A slow response to cultural shifts:** Younger Christians, especially Millennials and Gen Z, were engaging with faith content in new ways—through podcasts, YouTube channels, and digital study tools—yet bookstores remained centered on physical books and CDs.
- **A lack of strategic partnerships:** Instead of forging alliances with emerging Christian digital platforms, most bookstores remained siloed, missing opportunities to remain relevant.

Ironically, Christian publishing houses like Zondervan and Thomas Nelson adapted, leveraging digital distribution and e-books to stay afloat. The bookstores selling these products, however, did not.

4. The Case for Redeeming Innovation

The demise of the Christian bookstore sector is more than just a cautionary business tale; it is a warning about the dangers of disengaging from the future. The failure to futureproof was not due to a lack of faith but a lack of vision. There was an opportunity to reimagine what a Christian bookstore could be in a digital age—perhaps as a hybrid model blending physical and online presence, or as a content-driven platform that nurtured faith communities in new ways.

Some faith-driven entrepreneurs are now attempting to rebuild in ways that acknowledge the failures of the past. Online platforms like Faith-Gateway (owned by HarperCollins Christian Publishing) have created digital ecosystems that blend content, commerce, and community. Churches and independent authors have leveraged direct-to-consumer models to bypass traditional bookstores. These efforts suggest that the impulse to create faith-centered retail experiences is not dead, but it must be reborn in a form that aligns with contemporary realities.

Conclusion: Faith, Innovation, and the Need to Look Forward

Christian bookstores were not just victims of market forces; they were victims of a failure to innovate. The lesson here is clear: faith and innovation are not opposites. The biblical narrative is filled with examples of God's people adapting to new circumstances—whether it was Joseph using strategic foresight to prepare for famine, Paul leveraging Roman roads to spread the gospel, or the early church using the printing press to disseminate Scripture.

In an era of AI, digital disruption, and rapid technological change, the challenge for faith-driven enterprises is not just to survive but to lead. The failure of Christian bookstores should not be seen as an inevitability but as a missed opportunity—one that future faith-driven innovators must not repeat.

"The big challenge is to become all that you have the possibility of becoming. You cannot believe what it does to the human spirit to maximize your human potential and stretch yourself to the limit."

Jim Rohn – American Entrepreneur

CHAPTER 12
The Theology of Giftedness

"For the gifts and the calling of God are irrevocable."
Romans 11:29

In the opening chapters of Genesis, we are introduced to a God who creates. From the formless void emerges light, order, life, and beauty as God speaks the universe into existence. Genesis 1 and 2 are not merely accounts of creation; they are an invitation to see ourselves as reflections of a Creator who delights in doing new things.

When God declares in Genesis 1:26-28, "Let Us make man in Our image, according to Our likeness; let them have dominion..." He entrusts humanity with the responsibility to act like Him - to imagine, innovate, and steward creation. This dual reality, that God is the ultimate Creator and we are co-creators, forms a foundation for faith and engagement with the world.

Yet many people of faith struggle to reconcile these truths. Fear of "playing God" often leads to resistance to innovation and progress, driven by the mistaken belief that these are incompatible with faith. This chapter explores the theological foundation of giftedness, the tension of faith and innovation, and the urgent call for believers to embrace their role as co-creators with God in the age of rapid technological advancement.

Giftedness as a Universal Human Trait

The Imago Dei: The Foundation of Giftedness

Genesis 1:26-27 establishes humanity's creation in the image of God:

"Then God said, 'Let Us make man in Our image, according to Our likeness; let them have dominion...'"

Being made in God's image (imago Dei) bestows all humans with intrinsic giftedness:

1. **Reflecting Divine Creativity**: Every person carries the capacity for creativity, wisdom, and problem-solving, reflecting the nature of a Creator God. Giftedness is not reserved for an elite few but is woven into the fabric of humanity.

2. **Rebutting Narrow Views of Giftedness**: Educational paradigms often restrict giftedness to observable exceptionalities, but the imago Dei affirms that every individual carries extraordinary potential.

Giftedness is innate, not achieved. It is a birthright, reflecting divine intentionality. Whether expressed through groundbreaking technologies, artistic achievements, or everyday problem-solving, this universal giftedness attests to the Creator's design.

The Genesis Mandate and the Activation of Giftedness

Genesis 1:28 extends humanity's purpose:

"Then God blessed them, and God said to them, 'Be fruitful and multiply; fill the earth and subdue it; have dominion...'"

This mandate combines responsibility with the capacity to fulfill it. God's blessing activates innate abilities, empowering humanity to thrive and steward creation.

Key Implications:

1. **Empowerment through Blessing**: God's blessing reveals and activates latent potential. The capacity to create, steward, and innovate is part of our nature, amplified through His blessing.

2. **Technological Amplification**: In the age of AI, tools like robotics and digital platforms extend humanity's reach, enabling us to address challenges in ways previously unimaginable.

Even those who do not acknowledge God reflect this giftedness. Scientific breakthroughs, technological advancements, and artistic achievements demonstrate that all humanity shares in the divine image and mandate to build.

Co-Creators with God

The God Who Creates New Things

Genesis 1 and 2 are profound declarations of God's creative power. Over six days, He speaks life into existence: light and darkness, land and sea, plants and animals. Each act of creation is intentional, demonstrating order, purpose, and beauty. In Genesis 2, God forms man from the dust, breathing life into him—a deeply personal and intimate act.

When God declares humanity's creation in His image, He empowers us to act in His likeness. This is not a license for exploitation but a call to responsibility: to bring order out of chaos, to build systems that reflect His character, and to innovate for the flourishing of creation.

Psalm 82:6 declares, "I said, 'You are gods, and all of you are children of the Most High.'" Jesus echoes this in John 10:34, affirming humanity's divine authority and responsibility. Far from dishonoring God, creativity and innovation honor Him by reflecting His nature.

Can We Be Modern and Faithful?

A recurring question for believers is whether modernity and faithfulness can coexist. Can we drive Teslas, use iPhones, and leverage AI without compromising our faith? The answer lies in understanding that tools are not inherently evil; their value depends on their purpose and use.

Jesus came that we might have life and have it abundantly (John 10:10). Abundant life encompasses spiritual, physical, and emotional flourishing. Technology, when used responsibly, can enhance all these aspects, from improving healthcare to enabling global communication.

Rejecting technology out of fear is to miss opportunities to reflect God's creativity and compassion. True faith engages with the world, using the tools of each age to advance the kingdom and improve well-being.

Faith to Innovate: Courage in Uncertainty

Faith to innovate is characterized by a willingness to act despite uncertainty. Hebrews 11:1 defines faith as "the substance of things hoped for, the evidence of things not seen." This tension - the belief in what is possible without full certainty of the outcome - drives human progress.

Examples include:
- Scientists hypothesizing and experimenting.
- Entrepreneurs risking failure to build something new.
- Artists creating works without guarantees of success.

Overcoming Fear and False Humility

Resistance to innovation often stems from fear or false humility:

1. **Fear of Change**: The Pharisees rejected Jesus' new way out of fear of losing control. Similarly, fear blinds the faith community to the opportunities technology offers.
2. **False Humility**: Some believe success will lead to arrogance or distance from God, denying the truth of Ephesians 3:20: "God is able to do exceedingly abundantly above all that we ask or think, according to the power that works in us."

True humility recognizes that success reflects God's power, not self-generated effort. To refuse to innovate is to deny God the opportunity to work through us.

Toward a Theology of Technology

Stewarding the Tools of Our Time

God's mandate to steward creation includes the tools of our age—AI, renewable energy, and digital platforms. These tools are not threats but opportunities to fulfill our role as co-creators:

1. **AI in Healthcare**: Revolutionizing treatments and accessibility.
2. **Renewable Energy**: Addressing environmental challenges as stewards of creation.
3. **Digital Platforms**: Amplifying the gospel and connecting communities globally.

Call to Co-Creation

Genesis begins with a God who creates, and it invites us to join Him in that work. To be made in His image is to be empowered to imagine, innovate, and build. Faith and innovation are not opposing forces but complementary truths.

In the age of AI, believers have unprecedented opportunities to reflect God's creativity and compassion. By embracing our role as co-creators, we can build a world that honors Him and serves others. Fear may whisper its warnings, but faith calls us to step forward. The tools are here. The call is clear. What will we build?

Discussion Questions

On Giftedness and the Imago Dei

1. How does understanding the imago Dei (being made in God's image) influence how we view creativity and innovation?

2. What are some ways we can broaden our definition of giftedness beyond traditional notions of talent or skill?

3. How does recognizing giftedness as universal challenge societal or educational paradigms that prioritize exceptionalism?

On the Genesis Mandate

4. Genesis 1:28 calls humanity to "be fruitful and multiply" and to "subdue the earth." How does this mandate apply in the context of technological advancements like AI?

5. In what ways does God's blessing activate our capacity to create, innovate, and steward creation responsibly?

6. How can the faith community reconcile the tension between using technology to amplify human ability and avoiding the pitfalls of exploitation?

On Faith and Innovation

7. The chapter asks, "Can we be modern and faithful?" How do you personally navigate this question in your life?

8. What role does faith play in driving innovation, particularly when outcomes are uncertain?

9. How can fear and false humility hinder the faith community from embracing its role as co-creators with God?

On Theology and Technology

10. How can technology like AI, renewable energy, and digital platforms reflect God's nature and serve humanity?

11. What safeguards should the faith community implement to ensure technology aligns with Kingdom values?

12. How can the Church encourage members to embrace their giftedness and step into innovative roles without fear?

Practical Exercises

Personal Reflection

1. **Discovering Your Giftedness:**
   - Reflect on the ways you uniquely reflect God's creativity and purpose.
   - Write down three ways you can use your gifts to serve others and honor God.
2. **Faith to Innovate:**
   - Identify a situation in your life or community where innovation could make a positive difference.
   - Write a short plan for how you might approach this challenge with faith and creativity.

Group Activities

3. **Imago Dei Brainstorm:**
   - In small groups, brainstorm examples of how the imago Dei is reflected in diverse forms of creativity and innovation (e.g., art, technology, community-building).

- Discuss how these examples can inspire faith-driven action in the modern world.

4. **Faith and Technology Debate:**
   - Divide into two groups. One argues that technology is inherently neutral, while the other argues it is inherently dangerous.
   - Conclude with a discussion on how faith communities can discern the appropriate use of technology.

Strategic Planning

5. **Co-Creation Workshop:**
   - Plan a workshop for your faith community to explore ways members can embrace their roles as co-creators.
   - Include sessions on creativity, innovation, and practical tools for engaging with technology.

6. **Technology Stewardship Plan:**
   - Develop a plan for how your faith community can responsibly use AI, renewable energy, or digital platforms to serve its mission.

- Include strategies for training members and aligning technology use with biblical principles.

Vision and Implementation

7. **Innovation for the Kingdom:**
   - Identify a current societal issue (e.g., healthcare access, environmental sustainability) where innovation could reflect God's compassion and creativity.
   - Create a vision for how faith-driven innovation could address this issue.
8. **Theology of Technology Statement:**
   - Collaboratively draft a statement that outlines your group's understanding of how faith and technology intersect.
   - Include principles for using technology to honor God and serve others.

Skills for Faith and Innovation

9. **Creativity Activation Exercise:**
   - Choose a real-world problem in your community and brainstorm innovative solutions.

- Reflect on how these solutions reflect God's creative nature.

10. **Overcoming Fear of Innovation:**
    - Identify fears or barriers that might prevent you from embracing innovation.
    - Write down steps to overcome these fears, grounded in scripture and prayer.

"The God of the Bible is also the God of the genome. He can be worshiped in the cathedral or in the laboratory."

Francis Collins – American Physicist/Scientist

CHAPTER 13
The Symbiosis of Godlikeness and Godliness

"His divine power has given to us all things
that pertain to life and godliness, through
the knowledge of Him who called us by glory and
virtue, 4 by which have been given to us exceedingly
great and precious promises, that through these
you may be partakers of the divine
nature, having escaped the corruption
that is in the world through lust."
2 Peter 1:3-4

Introduction

From the beginning, humanity was created in God's image—a profound truth that imbues us with dignity, purpose, and the capacity to reflect divine attributes. This calling to bear God's likeness (*godlikeness*) is intertwined with the mandate to walk in reverence and obedience to Him (*godliness*). These two dimensions are not in conflict;

they are symbiotic. Together, they form the divine blueprint for humanity.

Yet this harmony is delicate. When godlikeness becomes untethered from godliness, ambition swells into destructive pride. Conversely, when godliness is reduced to self-abasement, it fosters a hollow religiosity that stifles creativity and meaningful engagement with the world. This chapter explores the balance between godlikeness and godliness—a dynamic partnership that empowers humanity to flourish, inspire, and redeem.

Godlikeness: Humanity as Divine Image-Bearers

Genesis 1:26 declares, "Then God said, 'Let us make mankind in our image, in our likeness, so that they may rule over the fish in the sea and the birds in the sky, over the livestock and all the wild animals, and over all the creatures that move along the ground.'"

To be godlike is to emulate the Creator by reflecting His attributes:

- **Creativity:** Mirroring God's inventive power in forming the universe.

- **Authority:** Exercising stewardship over creation with wisdom and care.
- **Relationality:** Building self-giving relationships, echoing the perfect unity of the Trinity.
- **Wisdom:** Using discernment to bring order and justice to the world.

Godlikeness equips humanity to innovate, create, and lead. Yet, it is not an aspiration to become God—it is a mandate to reflect Him.

Godliness: Reverence and Obedience

While godlikeness defines humanity's capacity, godliness defines its posture. As Moses asked in Deuteronomy 10:12, "And now, Israel, what does the Lord your God ask of you but to fear the Lord your God, to walk in obedience to Him, to love Him, to serve the Lord your God with all your heart and with all your soul?"

To be godly is to recognize God's ultimate authority and our dependence on Him:

- **Obedience:** Aligning human ambition with divine purpose.

- **Humility:** Acknowledging that, while we bear God's image, we are not God.
- **Worship:** Ensuring that the pursuit of godlikeness does not lead to idolatry.

Godliness anchors godlikeness, safeguarding creativity from devolving into destructive ambition and grounding humanity in reverence and gratitude.

The Tension Between Godlikeness and Godliness

When godlikeness and godliness work in harmony, they create a life of boldness and reverence, ambition and humility - a life that glorifies God and transforms the world. However, when either is pursued in isolation, the result is imbalance:

1. **Untethered Godlikeness:** Ambition swells into pride, leading humanity to overreach and usurp God's throne.
2. **Hollow Godliness:** Without transformative power, faith becomes a lifeless ritual, clinging to form without substance.

As Paul warns in 2 Timothy 3:5, there are those who have "a form of godliness but deny its power." This powerless faith diminishes humanity, offering no compelling vision for transformation.

Redeeming Humanity: Faith That Inspires and Transforms

Faith must integrate godlikeness and godliness to redeem humanity. This integration ensures that faith is both active and reverent, creative and humble.

1. **Godlikeness Redeems Creativity:**
   Godlikeness calls believers to engage boldly with the world's challenges, particularly in an age of rapid innovation. Faith communities must lead in ethical innovation, reflecting God's justice and creativity in areas like artificial intelligence, renewable energy, and digital technology.

2. **Godliness Redeems Purpose:**
   Godliness ensures that creativity serves divine purposes, aligning human progress with humility and worship. It invites believers to engage with the complexities of the modern world while staying rooted in God's eternal truths.

Godliness With Contentment

As Paul observes in 1 Timothy 6:6, "Godliness with contentment is great gain." Without contentment, godliness risks devolving into performative piety or self-righteousness. Contentment grounds ambition in gratitude, reminding us of our dependence on God's provision.

Together, godliness and contentment ensure that faith is neither restless nor rigid. They temper human ambition, anchoring it in humility and trust.

Avoiding Hollow Godliness

A faith that lacks power and purpose manifests as:

- **Legalism:** Reducing faith to rules devoid of relationship.
- **Passivity:** Retreating from the world rather than engaging with it.
- **Fear of Innovation:** Resisting progress out of fear of disruption.

This hollow godliness diminishes humanity, offering no vision for the transformative power of the gospel.

The Symbiosis of Godlikeness and Godliness

To fulfill its calling, the faith community must integrate godlikeness and godliness, creating a faith that inspires, empowers, and redeems. This symbiosis enables believers to engage boldly with the world's challenges while walking humbly before God.

1. **Steward Creation:** Leverage human creativity for God's glory and the world's good.
2. **Anchor in Reverence:** Ensure that all pursuits are guided by humility and obedience.
3. **Embrace Innovation:** See new technologies and ideas as opportunities to reflect God's image.

Conclusion: Fully Human, Fully Alive

Faith that integrates godlikeness and godliness does not retreat into ritual or nostalgia. It redeems humanity through creativity, humility, and transformative power. This faith inspires innovation without arrogance, fosters humility without passivity, and redeems without diminishing.

To embody this faith is to reflect the fullness of God's design for humanity - fully human, fully alive, and wholly committed to glorifying God in all things.

The choice is ours: Will we cling to powerless forms of godliness, or will we rise to the calling of a faith that restores and reshapes the world in the image of its Creator?

Discussion Questions

On Godlikeness and Godliness

1. How do godlikeness (reflecting God's attributes) and godliness (reverence and obedience) complement each other in the life of a believer?
2. What are the dangers of pursuing godlikeness without godliness, or godliness without godlikeness?
3. Genesis 1:26 calls humanity to bear God's image. How does this calling empower us to be creative, relational, and wise stewards of creation?

On Balance and Integration

4. Why is it important to balance ambition with humility and creativity with reverence?
5. How does 1 Timothy 6:6 ("Godliness with contentment is great gain") help anchor human ambition in gratitude and trust?
6. What does it mean to have a faith that "redeems without diminishing" and how does this apply to innovation and progress?

On Faith in Action

7. Paul warns against a "form of godliness" that denies its power (2 Timothy 3:5). What does this look like in modern faith communities?
8. How can the faith community lead in ethical innovation while staying grounded in God's truths?
9. How does contentment temper ambition and protect believers from overreach or pride?

On Innovation and Worship

10. How can believers embrace innovation as an act of worship while avoiding the pitfalls of idolatry or exploitation?

11. How can faith communities ensure that technological advancements serve both God's glory and humanity's flourishing?
12. What role does reverence play in guiding creativity and ambition toward God-honoring purposes?

Practical Exercises

Personal Reflection

1. **Balancing Godlikeness and Godliness:**
   - Reflect on areas of your life where godlikeness (creativity, leadership) might be untethered from godliness (humility, reverence), or vice versa.
   - Write down steps you can take to integrate these dimensions more fully.
2. **Contentment and Ambition Audit:**
   - Identify areas where ambition might have overshadowed contentment or where contentment has led to passivity.
   - Reflect on how you can align these areas with God's purpose for your life.

Group Activities

3. **Case Study: Ethical Innovation:**
   - Choose a current technological innovation (e.g., AI, renewable energy, healthcare).
   - Discuss how godlikeness and godliness can guide ethical use and implementation of this technology.
4. **Brainstorming Symbiosis:**
   - In small groups, brainstorm practical ways faith communities can integrate godlikeness and godliness in their outreach, leadership, and innovation.
   - Share your ideas and create an action plan.

Strategic Planning

5. **Vision for Ethical Innovation:**
   - Develop a vision for how your faith community can lead in ethical innovation while maintaining humility and reverence.
   - Include specific areas of focus (e.g., education, technology, social justice).

6. **Community Stewardship Plan:**
   - Create a plan for how your community can steward its creativity and resources for God's glory.
   - Incorporate principles of contentment, gratitude, and humility.

Vision and Implementation

7. **Manifesting Godlikeness in Innovation:**
   - Write a personal or group statement on how godlikeness can inspire ethical innovation in areas like AI, healthcare, or environmental stewardship.
   - Include practical steps for bringing this vision to life.

8. **Reimagining Hollow Godliness:**
   - Identify examples of hollow godliness in your faith community or personal life.
   - Brainstorm ways to infuse these areas with the transformative power of a faith rooted in godlikeness and godliness.

Creative Engagement

9. **Artistic Expression of Symbiosis:**
    - ◦ Create an artistic representation (e.g., painting, poem, song) that captures the harmony of godlikeness and godliness.
    - ◦ Share it with your group and discuss how it inspires your faith journey.
10. **Daily Practice Challenge:**
    - ◦ Commit to one daily practice that reflects godlikeness (creativity, innovation) and one that reflects godliness (prayer, humility).
    - ◦ Share your experiences after one week.

"Habits are the compound interest of self-improvement. The same way that money multiplies through compound interest, the effects of your habits multiply as you repeat them."

James Clear – author, "Atomic Habits"

CHAPTER 14
The Habits of Godlikeness

"Success is the sum of small efforts,
repeated day in and day out."
Robert Collier - American author

Introduction

To reflect the divine attributes of God, believers must cultivate habits that align with their calling as image-bearers. Godlikeness is not an innate state but a discipline, requiring intentionality and practice. These habits equip us to innovate, lead, and engage the world as stewards of God's creation. In this chapter, we outline seven habits of godlikeness—practical disciplines that enable believers to mirror God's character in their daily lives.

Habit 1: Creative Engagement

- **Scriptural Foundation**: Genesis 1:31 "God saw all that he had made, and it was very good."

- **Practice**: Embrace opportunities for creativity in work, relationships, and problem-solving. Reflect on God's creativity by crafting solutions that bring beauty and utility to the world.
- **Real-World Example**: A Christian entrepreneur, inspired by the conviction that people living with intellectual and developmental disabilities are children of God deserving of dignity and celebration, creates an innovative AI-driven app that helps users plan meals and cook with step-by-step guided instructions tailored to their unique needs but also integrates features such as grocery list creation, nutritional tracking, and voice-activated assistance. This solution empowers individuals to live more independently, fostering self-confidence and reducing the burden on caregivers. Through partnerships with local churches and nonprofit organizations, the entrepreneur ensures the app reaches those who need it most, embodying a commitment to service and innovation that reflects God's love and creativity.

Habit 2: Stewardship

- **Scriptural Foundation**: Genesis 2:15 "The Lord God took the man and put him in the Garden of Eden to work it and take care of it."
- **Practice**: Care for the environment, resources, and people entrusted to you. Make decisions that promote sustainability and justice.
- **Real-World Example**: A church takes the lead in neighborhood cleanups, organizing monthly events where members and local residents work together to clean parks, streets, and public spaces. The initiative includes providing tools and supplies, offering refreshments, and creating a festive atmosphere with music and games for children. By fostering a spirit of collaboration, the church builds bridges between diverse groups in the community, creating opportunities for meaningful conversations and relationships. Over time, the effort transforms neglected areas into vibrant spaces that families can enjoy while demonstrat-

ing the church's commitment to stewardship and love for its neighbors.

Habit 3: Curiosity and Lifelong Learning

- **Scriptural Foundation**: Proverbs 18:15 "The heart of the discerning acquires knowledge, for the ears of the wise seek it out."
- **Practice**: Cultivate a habit of asking questions, studying new fields, and seeking understanding to reflect God's infinite wisdom.
- **Real-World Example**: A Christian physician, motivated by a desire to integrate her faith with her medical practice, dedicates herself to lifelong learning in the emerging field of integrative medicine. She attends conferences, studies the latest research, and collaborates with specialists to explore holistic approaches to healing. By combining modern medical advancements with insights from Scripture on the body and soul, she creates wellness plans that address physical, emotional, and spiritual health.

Her practice includes free community seminars where she shares knowledge about healthy living from a faith perspective, inspiring others to see health care as an avenue to reflect God's care and compassion for humanity.

Habit 4: Self-Motivation and Initiative

- **Scriptural Foundation**: Proverbs 6:6-8 "Go to the ant, you sluggard; consider its ways and be wise! It has no commander, no overseer or ruler, yet it stores its provisions in summer and gathers its food at harvest."
- **Practice**: Develop the ability to work independently, setting goals and pursuing them diligently as an act of worship.
- **Real-World Example**: A single mother, abandoned by her support network and facing significant financial challenges, takes the initiative to launch a home-based catering business. Despite having no formal training, she dedicates herself to mastering recipes and building a brand that reflects her values of faith, family, and excellence.

She begins by serving meals to neighbors and local church events, eventually gaining a reputation for her creativity and quality. Leveraging online platforms and social media, she grows her business into a sustainable enterprise that employs other single mothers in her community. Through her perseverance and trust in God, she not only provides for her family but also creates a ripple effect of empowerment and opportunity for others.

Habit 5: Innovation for Good

- **Scriptural Foundation**: Isaiah 43:19 "See, I am doing a new thing! Now it springs up; do you not perceive it?"
- **Practice**: Approach challenges with a mindset of creating solutions that glorify God and serve humanity.
- **Real-World Example**: A faith-driven entrepreneur creates a technology-powered social enterprise to help disadvantaged communities access resources to navigate complex housing markets, combat predatory practices, and leverage opportunities for homeownership. The enterprise in-

cludes an "Equity JROTC," which leverages technology to equip public high school students from historically disadvantaged communities to thrive in high-opportunity neighborhoods and cities. The enterprise facilitates cross-sectoral partnerships with banks, realtors, mortgage companies, philanthropists, governments, and churches to resource the transitioning of individuals from the "non-economy" to the mainstream of economic activity.

Habit 6: Networking

- **Scriptural Foundation**: Ecclesiastes 4:9-10 "Two are better than one, because they have a good return for their labor: If either of them falls down, one can help the other up."
- **Practice**: Build connections and partnerships that reflect God's relational nature and facilitate collaboration for mutual growth and impact.
- **Real-World Example**: A faith-driven small business owner, seeking to expand her bakery while maintaining its mission to honor God, actively networks with oth-

er local businesses and faith communities. She joins a chamber of commerce, attends church-hosted business events, and builds relationships with farmers and suppliers. Through these connections, she establishes partnerships that provide her bakery with organic, high-quality ingredients at lower costs and create cross-promotional opportunities. Over time, her bakery becomes a hub for community events, offering mentorship to aspiring entrepreneurs and providing baked goods to support local charities. Her networking efforts reflect her commitment to serving God and her neighbors through collaboration and shared purpose.

Habit 7: Excellence in Work

- **Scriptural Foundation**: Colossians 3:23 "Whatever you do, work at it with all your heart, as working for the Lord, not for human masters."
- **Practice**: Pursue excellence in your vocation as a form of worship, striving to reflect God's perfection.

- **Real-World Example**: A Christian architect, driven by a vision of creating spaces that inspire and uplift, takes on the challenge of designing a community center in an underserved area. Despite limited funding, she collaborates with local artists and builders to incorporate sustainable materials and multifunctional designs. Her meticulous attention to detail and dedication to creating a welcoming, functional space results in a center that becomes a hub for education, worship, and community gatherings. Through her work, she demonstrates how excellence can glorify God and transform lives, inspiring others in her field to pursue projects that combine creativity, faith, and service.

Conclusion

The habits of godlikeness outlined in this chapter provide a framework for believers to engage the world as faithful stewards of God's image. By embracing creativity, stewardship, curiosity, initiative, innovation, networking, and excellence, we reflect the divine attributes and fulfill our calling to glorify God in all that we do.

Discussion Questions

On Cultivating Godlikeness

1. How does practicing creative engagement reflect God's image in our lives?
2. What are the challenges of maintaining stewardship in a world that often prioritizes convenience over care?
3. In what ways can cultivating curiosity help deepen your faith and broaden your impact?
4. Describe a time when you had to rely on self-motivation to achieve a goal. What role did faith play in your perseverance?

On Faith and Innovation

5. How can faith guide ethical innovation in areas like technology or community development?
6. What role does networking play in advancing God's kingdom through your work and relationships?

7. What does pursuing excellence in work look like in your current career or vocation?

Practical Exercises

Personal Reflection

1. Identify one habit of godlikeness you want to develop further. Create a plan for implementing it in your daily life this week.
2. Reflect on how your current work or studies reflect God's creativity and excellence. Write down one way to improve.

Group Activities

3. Form small groups to brainstorm ways to use innovation for good in your community. Present your ideas to the larger group.
4. Role-play a scenario where you must network to solve a community challenge. Discuss the experience as a group.

Creative Engagement

5. Design a project or product that addresses a specific need in your community while reflecting godlikeness.

6. Create a testimony or short story about how practicing one of these habits transformed a life or situation.

"It's not what we do once in a while that shapes our lives. It's what we do consistently."

Tony Robbins – Motivational Speaker

CHAPTER 15
The Habits of Godliness

"We first make our habits,
and then our habits make us."
John Dryden – English Writer/Poet

Introduction

Godliness anchors godlikeness, ensuring that our creativity and ambition remain aligned with divine purposes. These habits cultivate reverence, humility, and obedience, fostering a life of worship that honors God. This chapter outlines seven habits of godliness, providing a framework for spiritual growth and alignment with God's will.

Habit 1: Daily Worship

- **Scriptural Foundation**: Psalm 145:1-5: "I will extol You, my God, O King;
And I will bless Your name forever and ever.[2] Every day I will bless You,

And I will praise Your name forever and ever. [3] Great is the Lord, and greatly to be praised; And His greatness is unsearchable. [4] One generation shall praise Your works to another, And shall declare Your mighty acts. [5] I will meditate on the glorious splendor of Your majesty, And on Your wondrous works."

- **Practice**: Dedicate time each day to worship through prayer, song, or reflection, centering your heart on God.
- **Real-World Example**: A busy professional begins each morning with a worship playlist and quiet time with God.

Habit 2: Scriptural Meditation

- **Scriptural Foundation**: Joshua 1:8 "Keep this Book of the Law always on your lips; meditate on it day and night."
- **Practice**: Read and reflect on Scripture daily, allowing God's Word to guide your thoughts and actions.
- **Real-World Example**: A student journals insights from daily Bible reading and applies them in interactions with peers.

Habit 3: Prayerful Dependence

- **Scriptural Foundation**: 1 Thessalonians 5:17 "Pray continually."
- **Practice**: Cultivate a habit of constant communication with God, seeking His guidance and expressing gratitude.
- **Real-World Example**: A caregiver prays for strength and wisdom while managing the needs of a loved one.

Habit 4: Humble Service

- **Scriptural Foundation**: Mark 10:45 "For even the Son of Man did not come to be served, but to serve."
- **Practice**: Serve others selflessly, recognizing the divine image in those around you.
- **Real-World Example**: A church volunteer organizes community meals for the homeless.

Habit 5: Obedience to God's Commands

- **Scriptural Foundation**: John 14:15 "If you love me, keep my commands."

- **Practice**: Align decisions and actions with God's Word, even when it's challenging or countercultural.
- **Real-World Example**: A business owner refuses unethical shortcuts, trusting God for provision.

Habit 6: Gratitude

- **Scriptural Foundation**: 1 Thessalonians 5:18 "Give thanks in all circumstances; for this is God's will for you in Christ Jesus."
- **Practice**: Regularly express thankfulness to God and others, cultivating a heart of gratitude.
- **Real-World Example**: A family keeps a gratitude journal, sharing daily blessings around the dinner table.

Habit 7: Community Accountability

- **Scriptural Foundation**: Hebrews 10:24-25 "And let us consider how we may spur one another on toward love and good deeds, not giving up meeting together."

- **Practice**: Engage in a faith community for mutual encouragement, correction, and growth.
- **Real-World Example**: A small group prays and studies Scripture together, fostering spiritual accountability.

Conclusion

The habits of godlikeness and godliness are not mutually exclusive but complementary, creating a balanced and transformative faith. By embracing these practices, believers can reflect God's character while walking in reverence and obedience, fulfilling their divine calling to glorify God and transform the world.

Discussion Questions

On Daily Worship and Scriptural Meditation

1. What does daily worship look like in your personal life? How can you deepen this practice?
2. Reflect on a time when Scripture provided guidance or comfort in a challenging situa-

tion. How can you build a habit of meditating on God's Word?

On Prayerful Dependence and Humble Service

3. How do you ensure prayer remains a central part of your daily life, even when you are busy?
4. What opportunities for humble service are available in your community? How can serving others reflect God's love?

On Obedience, Gratitude, and Community Accountability

5. Share an example of a time when obedience to God's commands required sacrifice. How did it impact your faith?
6. How does cultivating gratitude shape your relationship with God and others?
7. What role does community accountability play in your spiritual growth? How can you foster this in your faith community?

Practical Exercises

Personal Reflection

1. Start a gratitude journal, recording three things you are thankful for each day this week.
2. Commit to meditating on one Scripture passage daily. Write down insights and pray over how it applies to your life.

Group Activities

3. Organize a community service project, such as a meal program or a clothing drive, and reflect on the experience as a group.
4. Create a prayer chain within your small group, assigning members specific prayer requests for the week.

Faith and Action

5. Identify one command from Scripture that you find challenging to follow. Create an actionable plan to live out that command this week.

6. Plan and host a worship night for your faith community, incorporating music, prayer, and Scripture reading.

"Alice came to a fork in the road. 'Which road do I take?' she asked. 'Where do you want to go?' responded the Cheshire Cat. 'I don't know,' Alice answered. 'Then,' said the Cat, 'it doesn't matter."

Lewis Carroll – Author, "Alice's Adventures in Wonderland."

CHAPTER 16
The Fork in the Road

"Two roads diverged in a wood,
and I - I took the one less traveled by,
and that has made all the difference."
Robert Frost – American Poet

Introduction

The evidence of faith-fueled innovation and transformation throughout history is plentiful. During a recent visit to Venice, Italy, I felt the same way I did when I first toured the city decades earlier. Venice is humbling, making even today's visionary feel like a mere pretender. Built on over 100 small islands in a lagoon in the Adriatic Sea, the city has no roads, only canals traversed by iconic gondolas, water taxis, and ferries, carrying millions of tourists each year to experience its Renaissance and Gothic palaces, the renowned Murano glass craftsmanship, and the charm of Venetian cuisine.

In Venice, you feel the *Eximia Potentia Visionis et Fidei* - the extraordinary power of vision and faith. Without modern tools to realize impossible dreams, the ancients had an unshakable belief in their God-given potential, a conviction that the little divinity of their humanity could bring forth extraordinary works.

The true gift (beyond the romance of a gondola ride, the richness of Sicilian ice cream, coffee at Piazza San Marco, and the unforgettable dinner of pizza and grilled bream at Ristorante Centrale) as my wife and I celebrated our 37th anniversary in this unique city in 2024 was a renewal and refreshing of our faith: the belief that nothing God calls us to do is impossible. The visioneering, the craftsmanship, the enduring faith of those who built this miraculous city upon the sea, leaving behind Renaissance and Gothic palaces and masterpieces like St. Mark's Basilica, these are things that preached and refreshed us the most. They did not abandon their work when they encountered challenges that would break us today, working tirelessly across lifetimes and often never seeing the finished work of their imagination but gifting future generations with their best.

On October 27, we witnessed the Venice Marathon in Piazza San Marco, where competitors from around the world gathered. Africans (Ethiopians) Abera Birtukan and Tilahun Abebe claimed victory in the women and men's races respectively, surrounded by tourists and worshippers celebrating mass in the Basilica.

I often say to our team at Kitchen Copilot: "Let's build one for the ages." Venice, where they didn't build just one but many, brings this vision to life. The economic significance for Italy today of what these ancient people of faith built is astonishing: Venice's GDP is over 25 billion Euros. Its tourism income exceeds 1.7 billion a year. It's a gift, built with significant contributions from people of faith, that continues to give generously to Italy and the world.

Elsewhere, the faith community stood as a beacon of innovation and transformation. They not only built enduring cathedrals, but cities that exemplified human ingenuity, and institutions of higher learning that pursued knowledge for the glory of God. These achievements, guided by faith, were not mere acts of devotion but declarations of purpose and power. Yet, today, the faith community finds itself at a perplexing crossroads.

Instead of leading, it hesitates. Instead of embracing innovation, it retreats into the safety of routine. The institutions it once founded - great cities, architectural marvels, and universities - now stand as monuments not of faith, but of secularism, sometimes openly hostile to the faith that birthed them. How did we arrive here? And, more importantly, how do we return to the path of relevance and impact?

This chapter is a call for the faith community to return to the fork in the road where it took a wrong turn. This is not merely a call to a historical place of influence but to a theological place rooted in the story of our origins, where humanity's purpose was defined. It is not a call to nostalgia or empty piety but to the bold, unadulterated faith that once built civilizations and inspired movements of lasting change.

The Fork in the Road: When Faith Lost Its Way

The moment the faith community turned away from its role as a driver of progress, it ceded ground to secular forces. Historically, faith and innovation were inseparable. Nimrod, though ultimately misguided, understood the power of collective vision to build something monumental. Later, the Israelites under Solomon constructed a temple that stood as a marvel of the ancient world, a testimony to the creativity God instilled in humanity.

But this call to create is more than a historical marker - it is rooted in the theological foundation of the Genesis narrative. In the opening chapters of Scripture, humanity is given a divine mandate: to "be fruitful and multiply, fill the earth and subdue it" (Genesis 1:28). This cultural mandate sets humanity on a course of stewardship, creation, and cultivation. The act of building, innovating, and shaping culture was woven into humanity's identity from the beginning.

When the faith community chooses routine over risk and preservation over progress, it turns away not just from a historical legacy but from the original theological calling to reflect God's creative nature in the world. At the fork in the road, the faith community chose comfort over challenge, routine over risk, and self-preservation over the divine mandate to steward creation.

Returning to Our First Love: The Call to Unadulterated Faith

Revelation 2:4-5 contains a striking message to the church in Ephesus: "Yet I hold this against you: You have forsaken the love you had at first. Consider how far you have fallen! Repent and do the things you did at first." This call to return to our first love is not an invitation to sterile religiosity but to a vibrant, transformative faith that overflows into every sphere of life.

First love faith is not passive; it is active, daring, and creative. It recognizes that God is not merely the author of our salvation but also the source of all innovation. It compels the faith community to step into its rightful role as co-creators with God, bringing His kingdom to earth through works of beauty, justice, and ingenuity.

Returning to our first love is more than a call to personal piety. It is a call to realign with the divine story of origins, where humanity was entrusted with the responsibility to reflect God's glory by building, planting, and innovating. It is a call to reclaim the mantle of leadership in areas where faith once led - education, art, technology, and governance. It is to embrace the audacity to shape culture rather than retreat from it, to create rather than critique, and to innovate rather than imitate.

Choosing the Road of Impact

Returning to the fork in the road requires a decisive choice: to move from routine to impact. Religious routine seeks to preserve the status quo, focusing on rituals and traditions that often lose their meaning over time. Impact, however, is rooted in the Great Commission - to go into all the world and make disciples.

The road of impact is a road of risk. It requires engaging with the drivers of change - technology, culture, and innovation - not as adversaries but as opportunities to glorify God. It demands a posture of humility to learn from the world while offering something greater: a vision of life and flourishing that only faith can provide.

1. Education as a Weapon of Faith

Just as universities once taught theology alongside the sciences, the faith community must re-enter the conversation on education. This is not about reclaiming institutions for their own sake but equipping future generations with a faith-driven framework for understanding the world. Faith-based education must be rigorous, addressing modern challenges with ancient wisdom, and unapologetically centered on truth.

2. Innovation as Worship

Innovation is an act of worship when it reflects God's creative nature. Faith communities must inspire and empower their members to lead in fields like technology, medicine, and the arts, seeing these as sacred callings rather than secular distractions. Imagine tech hubs and start-ups founded by people of faith, not to compete but to collaborate for the good of humanity.

3. Cities as a Reflection of the Kingdom

The great cities of history - Rome, Constantinople, Jerusalem - were built with faith as their foundation. The modern city can once again reflect the values of the kingdom of God when faith communities actively shape urban development, advocate for justice, and create spaces where human dignity thrives.

A Vision for the Future

Returning to the fork in the road means rediscovering what it means to be salt and light in the world. It means faith communities must no longer view innovation with suspicion but as a divine invitation to lead. This journey begins not with nostalgia for past achievements but with a return to the theological mandate of Genesis: to steward creation with excellence, creativity, and purpose.

This journey begins with repentance - a turning away from fear and apathy and a return to bold, unyielding faith. It continues with action: building schools that teach both science and Scripture, launching businesses that prioritize people over profit, and shaping culture through works of beauty and truth.

Ultimately, the faith community must reclaim its role as a builder of civilizations. Not for its own glory, but for the glory of God, who calls His people to be repairers of broken walls and restorers of streets with dwellings.

Conclusion: A Call to Rise

The road of impact is not an easy one, but it is the only road that leads to relevance and renewal. By returning not only to the historical fork in the road but to the theological place of origins - the story of humanity's first mandate - the faith community can rediscover its purpose and power.

This is the moment to choose: Will we cling to the routines that brought us here, or will we step boldly into the future, trusting in the God who makes all things new? The fork in the road is before us. Let us return, and let us build.

Discussion Questions

On Faith and Innovation

1. How does the historical example of Venice illustrate the extraordinary power of faith-fueled vision and innovation?

2. Why is the faith community often hesitant to engage with innovation and progress, and how can it overcome these barriers?

3. How does the Genesis mandate to "be fruitful and multiply, fill the earth and subdue it"

relate to the faith community's role in modern innovation and cultural development?

On the Fork in the Road

4. What does it mean for the faith community to return to the "fork in the road" where it chose routine over impact?
5. How does Revelation 2:4-5's call to return to "first love" faith challenge the Church's current priorities and practices?
6. What are the risks and rewards of moving from routine to impact in faith-driven innovation and leadership?

On Reclaiming Influence

7. How can the faith community reclaim its leadership in education, innovation, and city-building without falling into nostalgia or self-preservation?
8. What role does repentance play in the journey back to bold, unadulterated faith?
9. How can faith communities balance humility and boldness when engaging with drivers of change like technology and culture?

On Building for the Future

10. How can faith-driven innovation and education reflect God's creative and restorative nature?
11. What are some practical ways faith communities can actively shape cities to reflect the Kingdom of God?
12. How does the call to be "repairers of broken walls" and "restorers of streets with dwellings" (Isaiah 58:12) resonate with the faith community's mission today?

Practical Exercises

Personal Reflection

1. **Choosing the Road of Impact:**
   - Reflect on a moment in your life where you chose routine over risk.
   - Write down one step you can take to move toward impact in your faith journey or vocation.
2. **Rediscovering First Love Faith:**
   - Reflect on Revelation 2:4-5.
   - Identify areas where your faith may have become routine and how you can reignite a bold, transformative faith.

Group Activities

3. **Faith-Fueled Innovation Workshop:**
   - In small groups, brainstorm ideas for faith-driven projects in technology, education, or city development.
   - Share these ideas and discuss how they align with the Genesis mandate and the Great Commission.

4. **Analyzing the Fork in the Road:**
   - Identify historical or modern examples where the faith community chose preservation over progress.
   - Discuss how these decisions could have been different and what lessons can be applied today.

Strategic Planning

5. **Reclaiming Education's Role:**
   - Develop a plan for how your faith community can invest in education that integrates faith and modern knowledge.
   - Include strategies for equipping future generations to lead in innovation and cultural development.

6. **Vision for Building Cities:**
   - Create a vision statement for how your faith community can contribute to building or revitalizing urban spaces to reflect Kingdom values.
   - Outline steps to engage with local governments, developers, and residents.

Vision and Implementation

7. **Innovation as Worship Strategy:**
   - Develop a strategy for promoting innovation within your faith community as an act of worship.
   - Include examples of practical tools, programs, or workshops to inspire creativity and stewardship.
8. **Living as Salt and Light:**
   - Identify areas in your local community where faith-driven influence could bring transformation.
   - Plan a project that addresses one of these areas, incorporating faith-based values and innovative approaches.

Creative Engagement

9. **Building for the Ages Exercise:**
   - Write a short reflection or create a visual piece inspired by Venice or another enduring symbol of faith-driven innovation.
   - Share how this inspires your faith community to build for the future.

10. **Faith and Innovation Challenge:**
    - Commit to a week-long challenge where group members identify one way to innovate or take a risk in their personal or professional lives that reflects bold faith.
    - Share results and reflections at the next meeting.

The Steward's Touch

By gentle hands the world is kept,
Through care bestowed, its blessings swept.
The fields, the homes, the tools we wield,
Their quiet whispers beg revealed:
"Attend to us, and we will give,
The strength to thrive, the means to live."

A plow left rusted, dreams decay,
But polished bright, it clears the way.
A garden wild, untended, chokes,
Yet blooms anew with tender strokes.
Each thread of life, though faint, will weave,
A bond of care, its grace received.

The hearth will warm, the road will guide,
If nurtured well, not cast aside.
The vessel sails through storm and tide,
When stewards watch, their hearts allied.

The smallest acts, the simplest care,
Resound as prayers breathed
through the air.

For things are gifts, not ends in kind,
They guard, sustain, connect, remind.
Through tending them, our hearts align,
With sacred whispers, the divine.
To take good care is not mere chore -
It's love in motion, evermore.
-   **Noah Manyika** - 2024

CHAPTER 17
Restoring Redemptive Stewardship

"Take care of things, and
they will take care of you."
Shunryu Suzuki - Monk

As my wife and I wandered through the ancient streets and marveled at the grand architectural feats of Venice and Paris during our European trip, a shared realization crystallized: these masterpieces are not mere relics but enduring symbols of generational stewardship. The Louvre, with its timeless grandeur, and the Cathédrale Notre-Dame de Paris - constructed over nearly two centuries by countless dedicated hands - are monuments to the power of commitment across generations. Yet, they also confront us with an unsettling question: What testament to human ingenuity and divine vision, what legacy are we, the faith community, building today?

The restoration of Notre-Dame following its devastating 2019 fire is a triumph of modern ingenuity, compressing decades of work into five short years. Advanced technologies and innovative construction methods have made this possible, highlighting the critical role of human creativity and cooperation in preserving what previous generations stewarded with care. Yet, while these marvels inspire gratitude, they also underscore a broader truth: stewardship is more than preservation. It is about building anew, creating what will one day inspire and sustain future generations.

The Mandate of Creation

From the very beginning, humanity was entrusted with stewardship. In Genesis, God commands us to "fill the earth and subdue it" and to "have dominion" over creation—not as conquerors, but as caretakers who reflect His glory. This mandate to steward creation encompasses the physical world, human relationships, and the systems that shape our lives. Stewardship is not merely a call to protect what exists but a divine invitation to co-create, innovate, and cultivate flourishing in every sphere of life.

Tragically, much of today's faith community has neglected this sacred responsibility. While the world faces critical challenges, the church too often retreats into self-preservation or focuses narrowly on spiritual impact without engaging the broader mandate to steward creation. This neglect has left a vacuum, one that secular ideologies and institutions have filled, often with approaches that prioritize profit over people or convenience over care.

The Perils of Preservation Without Vision

The European monuments of faith are breathtaking, but as Frank Bruni observed, many have become "tourist-trod monuments to Christianity's past." They stand as physical testaments to what faith once inspired, yet too often fail to point toward a dynamic and living faith today.

The faith community must recognize that advancing God's kingdom cannot be achieved solely through preserving historical achievements. Preservation must serve as a foundation, not a ceiling. The glory of God is revealed not just in what has been built but in what is being built - lives redeemed, systems reformed, and cultures transformed through the creative, redemptive work of His people.

Redemptive Stewardship: A Call to Action

To reclaim our mandate, we must embrace a posture of redemptive stewardship - a stewardship that not only preserves but redeems. This means taking what is broken, neglected, or misused and restoring it to its God-intended purpose. It means stewarding not just the resources of the earth but the tools of technology, the creativity of human minds, and the power of relationships.

Redemptive stewardship is about:

1. **Building for Eternity**: Like the faithful builders of Notre-Dame, we must adopt a generational mindset, investing in works that will outlast us and glorify God.

2. **Embracing Innovation**: Advances in technology, like those that accelerated Notre-Dame's restoration, must be viewed not as threats but as tools to fulfill our mandate. Faith communities must lead in innovation,

leveraging new tools to solve the challenges of our time.

3. **Engaging Culture**: We must move beyond the confines of church walls, shaping culture through art, education, business, and governance.

4. **Restoring Creation**: From environmental stewardship to social justice, the church must lead in redeeming what has been damaged or destroyed by human sin.

A Living Testimony

It might be tempting to dismiss Shunryu Suzuki's call to "Take care of things, and they will take care of you" as a call to idolize material possessions. Yet, the reality is much deeper: "things" - buildings, fields, livestock, cars, and the like - truly sustain us when we steward them wisely. They provide shelter, nourishment, and utility, reflecting the principle woven into creation. Just as Adam and Eve were charged with tending and keeping the garden in Genesis 2:15, their care of it would have sustained them in return.

As I stood in awe of Europe's grand cathedrals, I realized they serve as more than architectural marvels. These sacred spaces were designed not only to inspire but to invite. Every stone, sculpture, and spire points heavenward, calling people to encounter the living God. In the same way, the works of redemptive stewardship today - whether in architecture, technology, or social systems - must serve as living testimonies of God's kingdom breaking into the world.

The time has come for the faith community to rise to its calling. We must move beyond the nostalgia of preservation to embrace the bold, creative work of redemptive stewardship. Only then will we fulfill our role as God's stewards, bringing His light and life to a world desperately in need of restoration.

In the words of Isaiah, "They will rebuild the ancient ruins and restore the places long devastated; they will renew the ruined cities that have been devastated for generations" (Isaiah 61:4). May this be our legacy - not just monuments of faith's past, but living, breathing expressions of God's redemptive power for generations to come.

Discussion Questions

On Stewardship and Legacy

1. How do the monuments of Europe, like the Louvre and Notre-Dame, reflect the faith community's historical commitment to generational stewardship?
2. What does the Genesis mandate to "fill the earth and subdue it" teach us about our responsibility as stewards of creation?
3. Why is it essential for stewardship to go beyond preservation and include innovation and building anew?

On Redemptive Stewardship

4. How does the concept of redemptive stewardship challenge traditional views of the faith community's role in the world?
5. What are some modern examples where redemptive stewardship can transform broken systems or neglected resources?
6. Isaiah 61:4 speaks of rebuilding ancient ruins. How can faith communities embody this call in today's context?

On Challenges and Opportunities

7. What are the dangers of preservation without vision, and how can faith communities avoid becoming "monuments to Christianity's past"?
8. How can technological advancements, like those used in the restoration of Notre-Dame, be leveraged to fulfill the faith community's mandate of redemptive stewardship?
9. How can faith communities engage culture in meaningful ways through art, education, business, and governance?

On Building for Eternity

10. What does it mean to adopt a generational mindset in stewardship, and how can faith communities inspire this in their members?
11. How can the works of redemptive stewardship serve as living testimonies of God's kingdom?
12. What legacy of faith and innovation do you hope to leave for future generations?

Practical Exercises

Personal Reflection

1. **Legacy Audit:**
   - Reflect on what legacy you are building in your personal and professional life.
   - Write down one step you can take to align your work or actions with a vision of redemptive stewardship.
2. **Redemptive Creativity:**
   - Identify an area of brokenness or neglect in your community (e.g., environmental issues, social systems).
   - Reflect on how you can contribute to restoring it as a steward of God's creation.

Group Activities

3. **Case Study on Notre-Dame:**
   - Discuss the restoration of Notre-Dame as an example of redemptive stewardship.
   - Explore how similar principles can be applied to challenges in your community.

4. **Brainstorming Redemptive Projects:**
   - In small groups, brainstorm potential projects that reflect redemptive stewardship (e.g., green spaces, technology for social good).
   - Present these ideas and discuss how to bring them to life.

Strategic Planning

5. **Generational Stewardship Plan:**
   - Develop a plan for your faith community to build projects or initiatives that will serve future generations (e.g., educational institutions, sustainable businesses).
   - Include steps for implementation and strategies for long-term impact.
6. **Technology and Faith Strategy:**
   - Create a strategy for how your faith community can use modern technology to advance its mission of redemptive stewardship.
   - Identify potential partners and tools to help achieve these goals.

Vision and Implementation

7. **Community Rebuilding Initiative:**
    - Identify a specific area in your community that needs restoration or renewal.
    - Create a vision and action plan for addressing this need, incorporating faith-driven principles of stewardship.
8. **Building Living Testimonies:**
    - Write a group vision statement for how your faith community can create works of art, architecture, or technology that serve as living testimonies of God's kingdom.

Creative Engagement

9. **Stewardship Reflection Art:**
    - Create an artistic representation (e.g., painting, sculpture, or poem) that captures the essence of redemptive stewardship.
    - Share your work with your group to inspire creative approaches to stewardship.

10. **Daily Stewardship Challenge:**
    - Commit to a week-long challenge where group members practice daily acts of stewardship, such as reducing waste, volunteering, or mentoring.
    - Share reflections and results at the next meeting.

Finishing Strong

The final mile, the toughest test,
A call to rise, to give your best.
Transitions shake, they bend, they mold,
Yet seeds of purpose lie in the fold.

The questions loom,
the doubts take stage,
"Where now my calling?
What's next in age?"
But faith's compass, though
storms may throng,
Points the way to finish strong.

Not as the end, but a canvas blank,
A place to pour what wisdom sank.
Fear of the new, of tech, of change,
Can bind the hands, can feel estranged.

Yet tools await, like clay, like stone,
To shape a future still your own.
Embrace the shift, the reinvention,
Let courage spark your new dimension.

For wisdom stored, when
shared, takes flight,
A beacon burning through the night.
So finish strong, your impact vast,
A legacy built to outlast the past.

Noah Manyika - 2024

CHAPTER 18
Finishing Strong

"Now therefore, give me this mountain
of which the LORD *spoke in that day;"*
Joshua 14:12

The final chapters of life and career often present some of the most daunting transitions. Layoffs, retirement, and other disruptions challenge not just our sense of stability but also our identity and purpose. For people of faith, these transitions can feel especially disorienting, as they may grapple with questions about their calling and God's plan for their future. Yet, with the right attitude and a willingness to embrace change, these seasons can become opportunities for reinvention and impact.

Unfortunately, many in the faith community miss these opportunities because of a misplaced fear of technology. Instead of viewing technology as a tool for finishing strong, they see it as a threat or an enigma they are ill-equipped to navigate. This fear fosters passivity, robbing them of the chance to leverage their accumulated wisdom and experience to create something new.

The Opportunity of Transition

When someone ages out of the job market, they are often left with questions about their next steps. While younger generations may have the advantage of agility and technical fluency, older professionals have something far more valuable: the benefit of experience and longevity. This accumulated knowledge, domain expertise, and relational network represent a treasure trove that can be leveraged for meaningful work and entrepreneurial success.

Wisdom as an Asset

Proverbs 16:31 tells us, "Gray hair is a crown of glory; it is gained in a righteous life." Experience and wisdom are not liabilities; they are assets that set older professionals apart. Over the years, they have developed:

- **Domain Expertise:** A deep understanding of their field, which gives them insight into its problems and opportunities.

- **Networks:** Relationships built over decades that can open doors to new ventures or collaborations.
- **Perspective:** The ability to see the bigger picture and make decisions informed by both successes and failures.

In a world where technology accelerates change, this wisdom becomes even more valuable. Experienced professionals are uniquely positioned to identify gaps that technology can fill and to develop solutions rooted in real-world understanding.

The Trap of Risk-Aversion

Yet, many people of faith in this stage of life fail to take advantage of these assets. Why? Because they become risk-averse, clinging to stability and fearing the unknown. This attitude can lead to missed opportunities to reinvent themselves or contribute meaningfully in new ways.

The Bible is full of examples of individuals who finished strong because they stepped out in faith rather than retreating in fear:

- **Moses:** At 80 years old, Moses could have settled for a quiet life tending sheep. Instead, he embraced God's call to lead Israel out of Egypt (Exodus 3).
- **Caleb:** At 85, Caleb declared, "Give me this mountain" (Joshua 14:10-12), demonstrating a willingness to take on new challenges even in his later years.
- **Paul:** Writing from prison near the end of his life, Paul affirmed, "I have fought the good fight, I have finished the race, I have kept the faith" (2 Timothy 4:7).

These examples remind us that finishing strong requires courage, adaptability, and faith in God's provision.

Technology as a Tool for Finishing Strong

AI, as discussed earlier, represents more than just a technological advancement - it is a tool that can amplify wisdom and extend influence. By leveraging AI-powered platforms, older professionals can bridge the gap between their wealth of experience and the agility of modern tools. Whether writing a book, mentoring others through online platforms, or identifying business opportunities, AI provides a means to multiply impact while leaving a legacy.

Opportunities include:

- **E-Commerce Platforms**: Platforms like Shopify or Etsy make it easy to start selling products online.
- **AI Tools**: Tools like ChatGPT can help create content, draft business plans, or conduct market research efficiently.
- **Freelance Platforms**: Websites like Upwork and Fiverr connect experienced professionals with clients who value their expertise.
- **Creative Projects**: AI-powered tools can help develop podcasts, videos, or online courses to share accumulated wisdom with a broader audience.

Opportunities in Tech-Powered Entrepreneurship

Many experts suggest that older professionals have a better chance of succeeding in entrepreneurship than younger people. Why? Because their domain expertise allows them to:

- Identify real problems worth solving.
- Develop practical solutions grounded in experience.
- Build trust with clients, investors, and collaborators based on their track record.

Technology lowers the barriers to entry for entrepreneurship:

- **E-Commerce Platforms:** Platforms like Shopify or Etsy make it easy to start selling products online.
- **Digital Learning:** Resources like Coursera and LinkedIn Learning enable older professionals to acquire new skills, such as coding or digital marketing.
- **AI Tools:** Tools like ChatGPT can help create content, draft business plans, or conduct market research efficiently.
- **Freelance Platforms:** Websites like Upwork and Fiverr connect experienced professionals with clients who value their expertise.

Learning to Embrace Technology

Psalm 92:12-14 declares, "The righteous will flourish like a palm tree... They will still bear fruit in old age, they will stay fresh and green." Staying "fresh and green" in a technological age requires a willingness to learn. Leaders of faith-based organizations can encourage this by:

- Hosting workshops to demystify technology and empower older congregants to use it confidently.
- Pairing older members with younger, tech-savvy mentors in the church to foster intergenerational learning.
- Highlighting success stories of older professionals who embraced technology to finish strong.

The Dangers of Fear and Paranoia

As explored in Chapter 3, fear of AI often stems from misunderstanding its nature and potential. However, believers are called to approach the unknown with a spirit of power, love, and sound judgment (2 Timothy 1:7). Rather than seeing AI as a threat, we should embrace it as a God-given tool to engage with the world thoughtfully and ethically, contributing to solutions that reflect Kingdom values.

Ecclesiastes 11:4 warns, "Whoever watches the wind will not plant; whoever looks at the clouds will not reap." Similarly, those who wait for the perfect moment to adapt or the ideal set of circumstances to try something new will never take action. Faith calls us to reject paralysis, choosing instead to move forward with purpose.

Fear can manifest in several ways:

1. **Demonizing Technology:** Viewing innovation as inherently evil prevents people from seeing its potential for good.
2. **Self-Doubt:** Believing that technology is too complicated or "for younger people" discourages learning and growth.
3. **Resistance to Change:** Clinging to old ways of doing things limits the ability to seize new opportunities.

Faith offers the antidote to these fears. "For God has not given us a spirit of fear, but of power and of love and of a sound mind" (2 Timothy 1:7). A sound mind recognizes that technology, like any tool, is morally neutral. Its impact depends on how it is used.

Practical Steps for Finishing Strong

1. **Leverage Your Wisdom:**
   - Identify the unique insights and skills you've developed over your career. How can these be applied to new ventures or shared with others?
2. **Embrace Lifelong Learning:**
   - Take advantage of online courses, workshops, or local classes to build skills that complement your expertise.
3. **Use Technology Intentionally:**
   - Explore platforms and tools that align with your goals, whether it's starting a business, mentoring others, or pursuing creative projects.
4. **Collaborate Across Generations:**
   - Partner with younger people who bring technical skills and fresh perspectives. Together, you can create solutions that draw on the strengths of both generations.

5. **Trust God's Provision:**
   - ○ Finishing strong is not just about what you can achieve; it's about trusting that God will use your efforts for His glory. Pray for guidance, take steps in faith, and be open to unexpected opportunities.

The Power of Finishing Strong

Finishing strong is about more than personal success. It's about leaving a legacy that reflects God's faithfulness and creativity. When people of faith embrace technology as a tool for reinvention, they demonstrate resilience, adaptability, and trust in God's provision.

Ephesians 3:20 reminds us that God "is able to do exceedingly abundantly above all that we ask or think, according to the power that works in us." That power doesn't diminish with age; it grows with experience. By stepping out in faith, leveraging accumulated wisdom, and embracing the tools of the modern age, believers can finish their careers - and their lives - strong, bearing fruit that lasts for generations.

Let us reject fear and paranoia, choosing instead to embrace the God-given tools of our time.

For it is not only possible to finish strong in the age of technology - it is an opportunity to glorify God and leave a lasting impact on the world.

Discussion Questions

On Transition and Purpose

1. How can faith communities support individuals facing career transitions, such as retirement or layoffs, in finding purpose and direction?

2. Proverbs 16:31 describes "gray hair as a crown of glory." How can the wisdom of experience be leveraged during times of transition?

3. Why is finishing strong important for leaving a legacy that reflects God's faithfulness?

On Technology as a Tool

4. How can technology empower older professionals to reinvent themselves or start new ventures?

5. What are some examples of how people of faith have used technology to amplify their impact in later stages of life?

6. How can faith communities encourage their members to embrace technology rather than fear it?

On Fear and Adaptability

7. Ecclesiastes 11:4 warns against inaction due to fear. How can this principle guide believers facing uncertainty about technology or change?
8. What role does trust in God play in overcoming self-doubt and resistance to learning new skills?
9. How can intergenerational collaboration between tech-savvy younger generations and experienced older professionals create meaningful outcomes?

On Finishing Strong

10. The Bible provides examples of individuals like Moses and Caleb who finished strong. What lessons can we learn from their stories about taking risks and embracing new challenges?

11. What does it mean to "bear fruit in old age" (Psalm 92:14), and how can this inspire those nearing the end of their careers?
12. How can faith communities cultivate a culture that values lifelong learning and adaptability?

Practical Exercises

Personal Reflection

1. **Legacy Mapping:**
   - Reflect on the legacy you want to leave behind.
   - Write down three ways you can use your wisdom and experience to impact others meaningfully.
2. **Overcoming Tech Fear:**
   - Identify one technological tool or platform that intimidates you.
   - Commit to learning how to use it, starting with small, manageable steps.

Group Activities

3. **Wisdom Exchange:**
   - Pair older members of your group with younger, tech-savvy individuals.
   - Facilitate a discussion where both generations share their strengths and learn from each other.

4. **Brainstorming Reinvention Ideas:**
   - In small groups, brainstorm ways older professionals can reinvent themselves using their accumulated wisdom and modern tools.
   - Share ideas and provide encouragement for those considering a new venture or project.

Strategic Planning

5. **Technology Empowerment Plan:**
   - Develop a plan for your faith community to offer workshops or resources that empower members to use technology for personal growth or ministry.
   - Include practical steps for implementation and outreach.

6. **Entrepreneurship Roadmap:**
   ○ Create a roadmap for older professionals interested in starting a business or nonprofit.
   ○ Highlight how they can leverage their networks, domain expertise, and technology to succeed.

Vision and Implementation

7. **Finishing Strong Initiative:**
   ○ Design a program for your faith community focused on equipping individuals to finish strong.
   ○ Incorporate elements like mentorship, technology training, and spiritual encouragement.
8. **Legacy in Action Project:**
   ○ Identify a community need that could benefit from the wisdom and resources of older members.
   ○ Plan a project to address this need, incorporating technology and collaboration across generations.

Creative Engagement

9. **Testimony of Transition:**
    - Write or share a personal testimony about navigating a significant career or life transition.
    - Highlight how faith and adaptability played a role in finding new purpose.
10. **Daily Action Challenge:**
    - Commit to taking one daily action to embrace a new skill, connect with someone for mentorship, or start a project that reflects God's faithfulness.
    - Share reflections and results at the next group meeting.

"If there is hope in the future, there is literally power in the present. When people have hope, they discover powers within themselves they never knew they had. They find the courage to take chances, to make a commitment, to break old habits, to take control of their lives, and to step out in faith."

Zig Ziglar – Author, Motivational Speaker

EPILOGUE
Beyond the Fork - Building the Future Together

"And I told them of the hand of my God which
had been good upon me, and also of the king's words
that he had spoken to me. So they said,
'Let us rise up and build.' Then they
set their hands to this good work."
Nehemiah 2:18

Introduction

The journey we've traversed in these pages has been one of profound introspection and daring vision. Now, standing at the threshold of the future, we must ask ourselves: what will we do with the truths we've uncovered?

The fork in the road discussed in Chapter 15 is not a single decision but a series of ongoing choices that define the trajectory of humanity. Every algorithm coded, every decision influenced by AI, and every interaction shaped by technology carries with it an imprint of our values. These choices are opportunities to either dehumanize or redeem, to act in the likeness of our Creator or to abdicate our stewardship. The question is not whether we will influence the future but how.

This chapter weaves together the practical insights from earlier discussions with a clear call to action, focusing on the potential of faith-tech partnerships as a catalyst for transformation. By addressing systemic challenges such as housing, education, and economic empowerment, these collaborations can bring redemptive solutions to the forefront, ensuring that innovation serves humanity and glorifies God.

Why This Matters Now

The Church has a choice to make, and time is of the essence. The algorithms shaping our world don't wait for committees to convene. The decisions being made in Silicon Valley, Shenzhen, and beyond will impact generations to come. As Dr. Jawanza writes, "When economies change, family structures change." The impact of technological change on families - the foundational unit of community, whether defined by geography or by a conceptual structure of belonging like the Body of Christ - is undeniable and profound.

Thankfully, like the story of Israel, ours is not finished. We may be under assault, but neither God nor we are dead. The pen is still in our hands.

Our mandate is clear: We are called to be repairers of broken walls, restorers of streets with dwellings, and builders of systems that reflect the justice, mercy, and beauty of God. This is our moment to reclaim the mantle of leadership and creativity that the Church has carried for centuries. It's our moment to ensure that the future is not just built but redeemed.

A Theological Imperative: Faith in Action

Isaiah 58:12 exhorts, "Your people will rebuild the ancient ruins and will raise up the age-old foundations; you will be called Repairer of Broken Walls, Restorer of Streets with Dwellings." This verse highlights the responsibility to rebuild and restore, ensuring that all people have access to stable homes and opportunities to thrive.

Faith communities, embedded in neighborhoods undergoing rapid change, are uniquely positioned to address these issues. However, they cannot do it alone. A partnership with technology companies can amplify their efforts, enabling faith organizations to advocate and provide tangible solutions. Together, they can tackle issues like hyper-gentrification, which displaces long-standing residents and robs them of stability and opportunities to build wealth.

Is This Not David, the King of the Land?

When David fled from Saul and sought refuge with Achish, the king of Gath, Achish's servant remarked:

"Is this not David, the king of the land? Did they not sing to one another in dances, saying: 'Saul has slain his thousands, and David his ten thousands?'" - 1 Samuel 21:11

This question could just as easily be directed at the faith community today, which too often seeks to shrink into the shadows. It is not enough to be frustrated that, like Achish's servant, the world sometimes recognizes the faith community's potential more clearly than the faith community itself does. The servant's question exposes a deeper issue: the faith community's failure to leverage its legacy of leadership to meet the demands of the present.

The call is clear - it's time for the faith community to rediscover its identity and purpose. Who we were - builders of hospitals, founders of schools, shapers of culture, and creators of systems that reflect divine justice and beauty - must inform who we are now. The Church is still God's chosen plenipotentiary, empowered and entrusted to act on behalf of our sovereign King. In this capacity, it retains the authority and responsibility to lead and serve. The Church is, in a sense, still "the king of the land," but it must rise to the occasion with faith, creativity, and courage.

Equipping Communities: The Role of Technology

The mandate of the faith community extends beyond telling **The Story**. It includes creating, innovating, and building, even in the age of AI. In partnership with the tech community, the redemptive work of the faith community can include building thoughtfully designed digital platforms like *TruParity-The Equity Track*, discussed in Chapter 8. These platforms could include:

- **Educate:** Provide interactive modules on financial literacy, the home-buying process, and strategies to build equity.
- **Assist:** Provide AI tools that match users with government programs, grants, or low-interest loans tailored to their needs.
- **Advocate:** Provide resources to help users organize against displacement and support equitable housing policies.
- **Connect:** Facilitate mentorship programs connecting first-time homebuyers with experienced homeowners within the faith community.

These platforms would democratize access to information, equipping individuals to navigate complex housing markets and combat predatory practices. Technology companies can ensure transparency and cultural sensitivity, creating tools that empower marginalized groups. Faith communities, in turn, can leverage their moral authority and grassroots networks to encourage participation and foster trust.

Building Bridges and Breaking Barriers

The success of this initiative depends on intentional collaboration. Faith leaders must actively promote these tools through workshops, services, and community events, emphasizing their alignment with spiritual values. Technology companies, for their part, must commit to designing platforms that are accessible and user-friendly, ensuring they truly meet the needs of disadvantaged communities.

This partnership transcends practical utility; it embodies the sacred call to "be Repairers of Broken Walls" in a world desperate for restoration. Bridging the gap between faith and technology enables the creation of thriving communities where stability and opportunity are accessible to all.

To achieve this, the faith community must recognize that among them are individuals anointed by God for this work - Software Engineers, company CTOs, and others with technical expertise. These individuals, like Nehemiah, can inspire action by proclaiming, "the hand of my God which had been good upon me, and also the king's words that he had spoken to me." This testimony can move others to respond with, "Let us rise up and build." And together, they will "set their hands to this good work" (Nehemiah 2:18).

The Fork in the Road: Choosing Redemption

The decisions we make at this juncture will define the legacy we leave behind. Will we retreat into passivity, allowing systemic inequities to persist? Or will we rise as co-creators with God, leveraging the tools of our age to bring His redemptive vision to life?

Faith-tech partnerships are a tangible expression of the Kingdom of God in action. They demonstrate that innovation and morality are not mutually exclusive but can coexist in powerful ways. By engaging with the tools of the age, we can transform not only individual lives but also entire systems and structures.

A Vision of Hope

The pace of life has quickened, but God's presence remains constant. The advances in AI and technology, though daunting, are not beyond His sovereignty. They are tools that, when used wisely, can magnify His glory and extend His compassion to the farthest corners of the earth.

The narrative of humanity and technology is still unfolding. The decisions we make, the values we uphold, and the courage we show in facing the challenges of the 21st century will determine the legacy we leave behind. Faith communities must embrace this moment with courage and creativity, recognizing that the future isn't a distant horizon—it's the choices we make today.

Conclusion: Beyond the Fork

"Redeeming Sundar" has been a journey of reflection, but it must now become a journey of action. American author and motivational speaker Zig Ziglar once said, "If there is hope in the future, there is literally power in the present."

Hope equips us with the courage "to take chances, make commitments, break old habits, take control of our lives, and step out in faith." To this, we add reason - the why behind our hope: God's finished work, Christ's redemption, and His call to abundant life (John 10:10).

Let us step boldly into the future, carrying with us the faith that transforms, the hope that endures, and the love that redeems. The age of AI is not the end of the story; it is a new beginning.

Call to Action:

1. **Collaborate Intentionally:** Faith communities and technology leaders must unite to address systemic challenges, ensuring that innovation serves humanity and glorifies God.
2. **Embrace the Theology of Giftedness:** Use your unique talents—whether in programming, teaching, or caregiving—to build tools that uplift, empower, and heal.
3. **Proactively Build the Proactive Kingdom:** Take bold steps to create systems, policies, and technologies that reflect Kingdom values of equity, justice, and love.
4. **Restore Redemptive Stewardship:** Advocate for ethical frameworks and ensure that the benefits of technology are shared equitably.

Together, as Repairers of Broken Walls, we can bridge the gap between faith and technology to build a future that glorifies God, serves humanity, and sets a lasting legacy for generations to come.

Discussion Questions

Understanding the Fork in the Road

1. The chapter emphasizes that the fork in the road isn't a single decision but a series of ongoing choices. What choices do you think the Church faces today in the context of technology and innovation?

2. How does the concept of "redeeming technology" challenge the way we typically view AI and other advancements? Share examples where innovation has been used redemptively.

Faith-Tech Partnerships

3. Isaiah 58:12 describes the role of "Repairers of Broken Walls." How can faith-tech partnerships embody this calling in addressing systemic challenges like housing or education?

4. Discuss the proposed digital platform outlined in the chapter. How could each feature (education, assistance, advocacy, and connection) impact disadvantaged communities? Are there additional features you'd suggest, particularly those emphasizing cultural adaptability?

5. What potential barriers might arise in implementing faith-tech partnerships, and how can they be overcome?

Choosing Redemption

6. The chapter frames this moment as a choice between passivity and redemption. What steps can individuals and faith communities take to ensure they choose redemption in their engagement with technology?

7. How can the Church's involvement in technology be a powerful witness to both believers and non-believers?

8. What steps can individuals and faith communities take to engage with technology responsibly and ensure its global impact aligns with Kingdom values?

Vision and Legacy

9. Reflect on the statement, "The story of humanity and technology is still being written." What role do you see for yourself and your community in shaping this narrative?
10. How does the idea of "proactive Kingdom building" resonate with you? What practical steps can you take to contribute to this vision?
11. What role do collaboration and shared expertise play in shaping a redemptive vision for the future? How can you foster partnerships in your own context?"

Practical Exercises

For Individuals

1. **Personal Fork in the Road**
Reflect on a personal decision where you're at a "fork in the road." Write down two potential paths: one that embraces faith-driven action and one that defaults to passivity. Pray for wisdom and take a step toward the redemptive choice.

2. **Communal Fork in the Road:** Reflect on a communal decision where you're at a 'fork in the road.' Write down two potential paths and consider how your choice could impact your community. Pray for wisdom and take a step toward the redemptive choice.

3. **Giftedness Audit**
   Identify your unique talents or skills (e.g., technology, teaching, caregiving). Brainstorm ways these can mentor others while addressing systemic challenges in your community.

4. **Case Study Reflection**
   Research an example of a successful faith-tech partnership or an innovation that addressed a societal need. Write a short reflection on what made it effective and how similar principles could apply to your context.

For Groups

1. **Design a Digital Platform**
   Divide into smaller teams and develop a basic concept for a digital platform addressing a systemic issue (e.g., housing, education, healthcare). Present your ideas to the group,

discussing how faith and technology can align in this project.

2. **Community Workshop Planning**
   Plan a hypothetical community workshop where faith leaders and technology experts collaborate to address a local challenge. Identify key topics, speakers, and outcomes you'd want to achieve.

3. **Barrier Brainstorming**
   Discuss potential barriers to faith-tech partnerships (e.g., mistrust, lack of resources) and develop action plans for overcoming one barrier within your local context.

Ongoing Challenge

1. **Proactive Kingdom Building**
   Commit as a group or individually to a project that reflects Kingdom values in technology. Document your progress over six months, sharing updates, challenges, and victories during regular check-ins.

2. **"Repairers of Broken Walls" Project**
   Choose a tangible issue in your community (e.g., homelessness, digital literacy) and collaborate with local faith groups and tech

organizations to create a small-scale solution. Track the impact and consider ways to scale the initiative.

the
issachar
coll3ctive
ENVISION · BUILD · TRANSFORM

JOIN THE MOVEMENT

Introducing The Issachar Coll3ctive

We are thrilled to introduce The Issachar Coll3ctive, a bold and transformative Faith-Driven Innovation and Impact Platform where technology, vision, and action converge to empower communities and inspire solutions to pressing global challenges. Inspired by the biblical tribe of Issachar - renowned for their understanding of the times and wisdom to act - the Coll3ctive is dedicated to bridging the gap between faith and innovation, equipping leaders and organizations to solve real problems while advancing Kingdom purposes.

At The Issachar Coll3ctive, we are about more than ideas. We're about action, impact, and transformation. Whether you are a business leader, church leader, entrepreneur, or student, this platform invites you to join a movement of faith-driven innovation that restores families, transforms communities, and amplifies the Christian witness in a rapidly changing world.

Why Coll3ctive with a 3?

The "3" in Coll3ctive represents the core pillars of our mission: Vision, Action, and Transformation. It's a reminder to think differently, create boldly, and lead innovatively. The stylized "3" reflects our commitment to modern solutions for timeless values and positions The Issachar Coll3ctive as a platform that unites faith, innovation, and action to meet today's challenges head-on.

Core Initiatives of The Issachar Coll3ctive

1. Faith-Driven Tech Hubs

One of the Coll3ctive's most exciting initiatives is facilitating the creation of **Tech Hubs** in faith-based organizations. These hubs will:

- Serve as centers for believers in technology to develop cutting-edge solutions for real-world problems.
- Provide opportunities for mentorship, equipping believers with the tools to innovate and lead in their communities.

- Empower churches to become engines of technological and social transformation, bridging faith and innovation in impactful ways.

2. The Issachar Coll3ctive Tech Challenge Board

The Tech Challenge Board will act as a platform for faith-driven innovators and organizations to propose, collaborate on, and implement solutions to some of the world's most pressing problems. This initiative underscores the faith community's commitment to providing visionary leadership in the age of innovation.

Launching Our First Challenge: Truparity - The Equity Track

We are proud to announce that Truparity: The Equity Track will be the first challenge featured on the Tech Challenge Board. This groundbreaking initiative addresses the knowledge and resource gaps that limit the psychosocial and economic integration of disadvantaged individuals into thriving societies. Truparity is more than a project; it is a vision for regenerative, faith-driven social enterprise.

Truparity's Core Pillars

- **Regenerative:** Solutions that renew and empower communities, creating lasting change.
- **Broadening and Deepening Knowledge:** Increasing awareness and understanding of systemic issues, particularly in housing and economic mobility.
- **Facilitating Cross-Sector Partnerships:** Engaging banks, realtors, mortgage companies, governments, philanthropists, and churches to maximize collective impact.
- **Timeless:** Addressing enduring needs with sustainable, forward-thinking solutions.
- **The AI-Powered Equity JROTC**

At the heart of Truparity is an AI-powered *Equity JROTC* program that equips public high school students from historically disadvantaged communities with:

- Education and resources to thrive in high-opportunity neighborhoods and cities.
- Mentorship and training to navigate complex housing markets and avoid predatory practices.

- Opportunities to access homeownership and economic inclusion.

Modeled after the transformative impact of the traditional JROTC, the Equity JROTC aims to transition families from the "non-economy" into the mainstream of economic activity, ensuring every family has the tools they need to flourish. Faith communities will play a critical role in this initiative, reinforcing the truth that God cares about every aspect of our lives and that the Church can lead the way in restoring hope and dignity to disadvantaged communities.

3. Faith-Tech Partnerships: Bridging the Gap Between Information and Action

In *Redeeming Sundar: Faith and Innovation in the Age of AI*, Dr. Noah Manyika writes about the importance of faith-tech partnerships to bridge the gap between information and action. The Issachar Coll3ctive takes this vision further by creating platforms for cross-sector collaboration and innovation. Initiatives like Truparity demonstrate how faith-driven leaders can step into global challenges with creative, technology-driven solutions, underscoring the critical role of faith communities in leading transformative change.

4. The Issachar Coll3ctive Media

The Issachar Coll3ctive Media is dedicated to telling the stories in film and other media that inspire and celebrate innovation and faith. Through compelling narratives, documentaries, and creative storytelling, it showcases how faith-driven innovation is transforming lives and advancing the Kingdom.

The Sounds of Issachar

Under this label, The Issachar Coll3ctive Media will release music that uplifts and inspires, including "Songs in the Key of Faith" - a collection of music rooted in faith, resilience, and hope.

Opportunities for Engagement

The Issachar Coll3ctive is not just a platform - it's a movement. Here's how you can engage:

1. **Faith-Driven Tech Hubs**
   Partner with us to establish Tech Hubs at your church, equipping believers to innovate and mentor others.

2. **Speaking Engagements and Workshops**
Book Dr. Noah Manyika or other transformational leaders for:
   ◦ Conferences and summits
   ◦ Church leadership retreats
   ◦ Board retreats for faith-driven businesses
   ◦ Seminary workshops
3. **Creating Issachar Coll3ctive Clubs**
Launch grassroots movements in your church, school, or organization with **Issachar Coll3ctive Clubs** that empower local leaders to engage in innovative problem-solving.
4. **The Tech Challenge Board**
Propose or collaborate on solutions for global challenges through the Tech Challenge Board, and be part of creating life-changing innovations.
5. **Resources and Merchandise**
Explore books, courses, music, films and merchandise by Dr. Noah Manyika and other global thought leaders, designed to inspire and equip faith-driven innovators.

Join the Movement

At The Issachar Coll3ctive, we believe that faith-driven innovation is not just about solving problems; it's about transforming lives, restoring communities, and advancing the Kingdom. Together, we can create a future where faith and technology converge to reflect God's heart for justice, mercy, and renewal.

Visit us at IssacharColl3ctive.com - yes, with a "3"! If you accidentally type **IssacharCollective.com**, don't worry - we've got you covered. You'll still find your way to us.

For inquiries and to book Dr. Noah Manyika for speaking engagements, email **info@IssacharColl3ctive.org**.

Booking Dr. Noah Manyika can also be done by completing a Booking Form on the Engagement Section of our website: www.issacharcoll3ctive.com

Be part of the change. *Envision. Build. Transform.*

About the author

Dr. Noah Manyika is a visionary thought leader, author, and dynamic speaker with over 30 years of experience in transformational community development and global social entrepreneurship. A Fulbright Scholar and former Senior Fellow with the Sagamore Institute, he holds a Master of Science in Foreign Service from Georgetown University's prestigious School of Foreign Service, where he studied under former U.S. Secretary of State Madeleine Albright. He also holds a BA in Journalism and Political Science from Romania's Academia Ștefan Gheorghiu, earned during the Cold War, a PhD in Christian Leadership from Vision University, and a Doctorate in Transformational Leadership from Bakke Graduate University.

His leadership journey began in Zimbabwe, where he held executive business and ministerial leadership roles from 1987 to 1994. After relocating to Charlotte, North Carolina, he founded Nexus Global Serve/Nexus Ministries, leading transformative programs and public-private partnerships to serve inner-city communities. His visionary projects included the Charlotte Children's Scholarship Fund, Brookstone School, and the Charlotte Empowerment Zone. In Zimbabwe, his One Tribe Problem Solvers Clubs facilitated partnerships with civic, business, and government organizations, earning him an invitation to advise the cabinet-level Organ for National Healing, Reconciliation, and Integration during a pivotal period in the nation's history.

Dr. Manyika has served on the Affordable Housing Cabinet established by the late developer John Crosland, Queens University's Advisory Board, and multiple boards, including United World Missions, Harvests of Hope, and Above and Beyond. He is the former Africa Chairman of Kalahari Capital Partners, an investment platform that combined new business creation with short-term trade finance projects in emerging markets.

A candidate in Zimbabwe's 2018 presidential elections, his diverse personal and professional experiences across Africa, Eastern Europe, and the United States have provided him with unique multidisciplinary insights into leadership, global engagement, and transformational change.

Currently, as the founder and CEO of Kitchen Copilot Inc., Dr. Manyika continues to innovate at the intersection of faith and technology, creating tools designed to empower families and communities. He is the author of *The Challenge of Leadership: Is There Not a Cause?*, widely utilized in Bible schools, churches, and leadership training programs.

Rooted deeply in faith, Dr. Manyika exemplifies his commitment to God's redemptive vision in both his professional and personal life. He shares this journey with his wife, Phillis, and their three children.

In his latest book, *Redeeming Sundar: Faith and Innovation in the Age of AI*, he calls readers to embrace their role as co-creators with God, leveraging modern transformative tools to shape a future aligned with His redemptive purposes. This book, along with "The Issachar Coll3ctive" (Issacharcoll3ctive.com) launching simultaneously, serves as a rallying call for Christian leaders, social entrepreneurs, and believers to approach the challenges of the modern world with courage, creativity, and conviction.

www.ingramcontent.com/pod-product-compliance
Lightning Source LLC
Chambersburg PA
CBHW071318210326
41597CB00015B/1266